IMAGES
of America

MILWAUKEE JAZZ

Loretta Whyte, one of Milwaukee's first jazz stars, is pictured at the Flame nightclub. A St. Louis native born Loretta Estelle Simpson, Whyte was a self-taught prodigy who was accompanying silent films by the age of 14. She moved to Chicago and then Milwaukee with her first husband, a banjo and violin player named William White. She met her second husband, James "Derby" Thomas, in 1932. Derby was a Milwaukee promoter, and together, they opened the Flame nightclub around 1945. The Flame was one of the hottest clubs in Milwaukee. Whyte led the house band at the Flame and hosted icons such as Duke Ellington and Count Basie. (Courtesy of the Wisconsin Black Historical Society.)

ON THE COVER: A faculty band from the jazz program at the Wisconsin Conservatory of Music poses at the Conservatory Recital Hall in 1977. From left to right are Eddie Baker (piano), Manty Ellis (guitar), Harold Miller (bass), Berkeley Fudge (flute), and Sam Belton (drums). This was a promotional photograph for the Jazz From the Conservatory concert series, specifically for a performance at the Milwaukee Art Center. Hattush Alexander was also billed on the show, though he is not pictured. (Courtesy of the Wisconsin Conservatory of Music.)

IMAGES
of America

MILWAUKEE JAZZ

Joey Grihalva

ARCADIA
PUBLISHING

Published by Arcadia Publishing
Charleston, South Carolina

Printed in the United States of America

Library of Congress Control Number: 2018961504

For all general information, please contact Arcadia Publishing:
Telephone 843-853-2070
Fax 843-853-0044
E-mail sales@arcadiapublishing.com
For customer service and orders:
Toll-Free 1-888-313-2665

Visit us on the Internet at www.arcadiapublishing.com

To all the cats who have ever called Milwaukee home,
and to those who carry this legacy forward.

CONTENTS

FOREWORD

When Joey asked me to write the foreword for this pictorial account of jazz in Milwaukee, I thought, "Wow, I might get famous!" Then I thought, "You must already have some level of fame or he would not have come to you." Mostly, I feel honored that after hearing my myriad stories, Joey felt I would be a good fit.

From the beginning, it was obvious that this was a labor of love for Joey. I also saw that he wanted to produce an authentic representation of the Milwaukee jazz scene from the perspective of the people who lived that history. I am so glad and proud to be among them.

My entry into the Milwaukee jazz scene came in 1979 by an odd twist of fate. As a result of doing a service for a friend, I ended up "sitting in" at the Jazz Gallery with a fledgling Sunday afternoon house band consisting of David Hazeltine on piano, Skip Crumby-Bey on bass, Scott Napoli on drums, and Brian Lynch on trumpet. Buddy Montgomery, who happened to be in the audience, decided I was worth mentoring and took me on the road as the band's emcee until he felt I was ready to handle the job of vocalist. When Buddy left for the West Coast, I teamed up with Melvin Rhyne, organist extraordinaire, whom I met through Buddy and his beloved Rosie Curro.

For the next 30 years, I lived between Chicago and Milwaukee and built performing careers in both cities, often blending musicians from each community. I discovered that even though Chicago is much larger, the dynamics for black musicians are pretty much the same. The love and camaraderie that jazz artists black, white, male, female, performer, club owner, young and old experience as we build relationships are indelible and, most of the time, joyful because we love this "great black music" as Duke Ellington called it.

I would like to give personal honor to the mentors and peers who made the difference for me. There are too many names to fit on this page, but a little birdy told me that Joey has put together a supplementary book that includes interviews, anecdotes, and additional pictures, plus my list of mentors and peers, so make sure to check that out too.

Thanks for the memories, Joey.

Forever grateful,
Adekola (Ifadunmade) Adedapo

ACKNOWLEDGMENTS

It starts with Tarik Moody, a great DJ and my boss at 88Nine Radio Milwaukee. Tarik gave me the original assignment that led to this book. From there, I must tip my hat to Jamie Breiwick, the "OG" of the Milwaukee jazz history archive game. The Milwaukee Jazz Vision, which Breiwick cofounded with Kevin Hayden, Neil Davis, and Steve Peplin, has been absolutely invaluable. I am indebted to Ben Barbera at the Milwaukee County Historical Society for securing photographs and for his dissertation "An Improvised World: Jazz and Community in Milwaukee, 1950–1970." That paper, along with Kurt Dietrich's *Wisconsin Riffs: Jazz Profiles from the Heartland* and Derek Pinkham's *Lives & Lessons of Musicians from the Cream City* are the building blocks upon which this book was constructed. Special thanks are also due to Jamila and Clayborn Benson at the Wisconsin Black Historical Society, Mark Davis at the Wisconsin Conservatory of Music, Jennifer Pahl at the Milwaukee Public Library, and Rufus King High School volunteers Houa and Choua Thao.

To all the musicians, their kin, and those in the scene who invited me into their lives and homes, their generosity and enthusiasm made this book possible. Much respect and gratitude go to Manty Ellis, Chuck LaPaglia, Adekola Adedapo, Neal Chandek, Al Jarreau, Howard Austin, Charles Queen, Leslie Johnson, Stacey Vojvodich, Kaye Berigan, Rick Aaron, Billy Johnson, Connie Grauer, Mark Davis, Jeff Hamann, Sam Belton, Tina Moore, Jerry Grillo, Dewey Gill, Ray Sherman, Pat Robinson, Aaronetta Anderson, Kevin Lynch, Bobby Tanzillo, Dustin Wittmann, Leslie Heinrichs, Glenn Kleiman, Jordan Lee, Steve Tilton, and Justin Thomas Brown.

My work would not be possible without the love and support of my family and friends. Extra special thanks go to my incredible fiancée, Kristina; her beautiful children, Julien and Vera; my parents, Mary and Fred; my brother Brent and his wife, Siobhan; and my friend Jamal Miller. Since I was born in 1985 to parents who love rock and roll and grandparents who listened to classical and polka, I must thank Q-Tip, Phife Dawg, and Ali Shaheed Muhammad for introducing me to jazz. Little did I know just how much we got in Milwaukee.

This book is but a slice of that history. I could only find so many photographs, talk to so many people, and include so much information. And so, I would like to acknowledge every soul that has ever been a part of the Milwaukee jazz scene but is not in this book.

INTRODUCTION

Several years ago, I embarked on a project documenting the history of what I consider to be the under-recognized jazz scene in Milwaukee, Wisconsin. It was a reaction to the severe lack of evidence online and elsewhere of Milwaukee's rich and storied jazz past. Important musicians such as Berkeley Fudge, Hattush Alexander, Manty Ellis, Penny Goodwin, Tony King, Will Green, Jessie Hauck, Bob Hobbs, and Dick Smith, to name a few, laid the foundation that would inspire generations of local jazz artists.

Not unlike other Midwest cities of comparable size and stature, such as Detroit, Chicago, and Cleveland, Milwaukee has struggled with many of the same societal problems: deep segregation, the decline of the working class, unemployment, poverty, underfunded education systems, and institutionalized racism. Milwaukee, a microcosm of America at large, has all but ignored its most important black cultural entities. This is evidenced by the decimation of Milwaukee's historic black district for the construction of the interstate in the late 1950s in the name of "urban renewal."

Oftentimes, the evidence is hiding in plain sight. Buildings you may have driven past hundreds of times and paid no attention to contain the echoes of American music and entertainment icons. The Ron-De-Voo Ballroom, which hosted the legendary Billie Holiday for four consecutive nights in August 1953 is one example. The Ron-De-Voo still stands at 1118–1126 North Avenue; however, it is hidden by decades of decay and neglect.

The original Milwaukee Jazz Gallery (926 East Center Street) was owned and operated by jazz warrior Chuck LaPaglia. The gallery ran international-caliber programming from 1978 to 1984 in Milwaukee's Riverwest neighborhood. Currently operated by the Riverwest Artist Association (RAA), and thanks to a partnership between the RAA and the Milwaukee Jazz Vision, the space has been revitalized into a community art/music venue once again. The Jazz Gallery Center for the Arts has embraced and honored its past and is now thriving in part because of that heritage.

Much of the driving force of the Milwaukee Jazz Vision (and this book) has been to shed some light on the contributions of the unsung heroes, the unrecognized masters, and the regional icons of past and present. My hope is that this book will not just be a nostalgic look at our rich past, but a compass pointing to what might be possible in our future.

Jamie Breiwick

One

IN THE DAY

Like America itself, jazz music is the result of various musical, spiritual, and sociological ingredients. Geographically speaking, jazz was born in New Orleans. It soon traveled up the Mississippi River and into the heart of the Midwest. Chicago became a breeding ground of jazz talent. Not long after, the music spilled north and made its way to Milwaukee, Wisconsin, where it has had a home ever since.

Milwaukee was known as a music center before jazz came to town. Between 1840 and 1860, there were orchestras in Milwaukee that could rival those on the East Coast. At the turn of the 20th century, daily opera performances were held in Schlitz Park, which opened in 1884 at Seventh and Walnut Streets.

John H. Wickliffe and his Famous Ginger Band of Chicago first brought jazz music to Milwaukee in 1916, just as the term "jazz" (or "jass") was being popularized. The band played at Schlitz Park, the first black group to do so. The Famous Ginger Band played so often in Milwaukee that some of its members moved to town, including bandleader Roy Wolfscale and his wife.

While jazz could be seen in downtown hotels and ballrooms around town, the hottest rooms were in the black neighborhood of Bronzeville. Located just north of downtown, most Bronzeville clubs were known as "black and tans" because they welcomed both black and white patrons. Even before clubs and bars began hosting jazz, Fourth Street School, Lapham Park Social Center, and the Booker T. Washington YMCA were centers of black social life where jazz was played.

Between 1920 and 1930, the number of musicians and music teachers in Milwaukee increased more than any other profession. In 1924, black musicians in Milwaukee formed their own union after being excluded from the local American Federations of Musicians union.

The first venue to specifically offer jazz music in Milwaukee was Club Metropole, which opened in 1922. The Blue Room and Congo Club opened in the late 1920s. Many more clubs opened between the 1930s and 1950s, including the Flame, Curro's, the Moon Glow, Thelma's Back Door, and the Celebrity Club, among others.

Photographs in this chapter include images from the earliest days of jazz through the 1950s with attention to both local and national performers.

Members of the Lapham Park Social Center Men's Band are pictured in the 1920s. The social center was an important place for the black community in the early part of the 20th century. Local jazz icon Manty Ellis remembers playing his earliest gigs there with saxophonist Bunky Green in a group called the Rhythm Kings. Legendary vocalist Al Jarreau also remembers singing at the social center as a kid. (Courtesy of Paul Geenen.)

The Clement Musical Club jazz band is pictured in front of an unknown building in the late 1910s or early 1920s. At this point, jazz was a brand-new art form, evolving out of ragtime, the blues, African rhythms, and classical music components. (Courtesy of the Historic Photo Collection/ Milwaukee Public Library.)

For many, Walnut Street was the epicenter of early jazz in Milwaukee. The corridor from North Third Street to North Twelfth Street, plus adjacent side streets, made up the heart of the black business and entertainment district. At its peak, there were a dozen or so clubs in the area with live music almost every night of the week. The Regal Theater, seen in this charcoal drawing, hosted live entertainment after the late movie on Friday and Saturday nights. These showcases were a training ground for local jazz musicians like Willie Pickens, Mary Young, and Billy Wallace. (Courtesy of Paul Geenen/Sylvester Sims.)

The Van Lanes Orchestra is pictured in Milwaukee in 1928. Many early jazz bands incorporated the banjo, a holdover from ragtime music. (Courtesy of Paul Geenen.)

Racine native Tommy Fox was a Milwaukee mainstay during the early days of jazz. Here, he is pictured with His Clever Little Foxes at the Congo Club in 1929. Milwaukee's preeminent female jazz star, Loretta Whyte, was a member of the Clever Little Foxes and is pictured (far left) at the piano. Local jazz guitarist Manty Ellis remembers his father Grover Ellis playing piano with Tommy Fox. (Courtesy of the Wisconsin Black Historical Society.)

Loretta Whyte is pictured performing at a club in the Bronzeville neighborhood. Whyte, a St. Louis native, was one of the premier organists in town, working at clubs, hotels, and even Borchert Field, the main baseball venue in town from 1888 until 1952. In the upper left is a banner for the Musicians' Protective Union Local 587, Milwaukee's black musicians' union founded in 1924. (Courtesy of the Wisconsin Black Historical Society.)

Legendary bandleader Duke Ellington is pictured hanging out with members of the Milwaukee jazz scene. Ellington is looking at local pianist Loretta Whyte. This photograph was likely taken at the 10-year anniversary party for the Flame nightclub, which Whyte co-owned with her husband, Derby Thomas. (Courtesy of the Wisconsin Black Historical Society.)

Minette D. Wilson, better known as "Satin Doll," was a staple of the Milwaukee jazz scene. Wilson was born in Mississippi in 1937 and moved to Milwaukee as a young adult. She is best known for dancing at the Flame nightclub and on tour with Duke Ellington. Wilson claimed that Ellington's song "Satin Doll" was named after her. She is pictured with her husband, Crickett, another well-known Milwaukee dancer. (Courtesy of Mary Young/Paul Geenen.)

An unidentified dancer is pictured performing at the Flame. Dancers would regularly accompany jazz musicians at nightclubs during the 1920s and into the 1960s. One newspaper advertisement for the Flame highlights the "Fabulous Shake Artist" Satin Doll, who regularly danced at the Flame. The club was located at 1315 North Ninth Street. (Courtesy of the Wisconsin Black Historical Society.)

Duke Ellington is pictured hanging out with members of the Milwaukee jazz scene. The three women kneeling are, from left to right, Mattie Belle Woods, Satin Doll, and Loretta Whyte. Crickett, Satin Doll's husband, is second from the right. (Courtesy of the Wisconsin Black Historical Society.)

Satin Doll is pictured with her husband, Crickett, and "Pumpkin." In 1977, Wilson opened Satin Doll's Lounge at 2337 West Fond Du Lac Avenue, an after-hours club. Local columnist William Janz described Satin Doll in a 1996 article: "One of our city's most memorable barkeeps . . . an attractive, sometimes regal, sometimes elegant, often shocking woman who can rattle your teeth with a flurry of words or a piece of a tree." (Courtesy of the Wisconsin Black Historical Society.)

William Edward Johnson, better known as "Scat" Johnson, was a pioneering singer and entertainer. He was born in 1915 in Leavenworth, Kansas, and grew up in Bedford, Indiana. Johnson was raised by his grandparents who ran a rooming house where black entertainers would stay, including Fats Waller and Billie Holiday. Johnson went to high school in Indianapolis. As a teenager, he was tap dancing in the streets for money. He was recruited in a touring minstrel show called Brown Skinned Revue, where he was known as "Rhythm" Johnson. (Courtesy of Leslie Johnson.)

Scat Johnson is pictured second from the left with Everett Clark on guitar, Jack Rice on bass, and Bobby Burdett on saxophone. Johnson came to Milwaukee for a gig in 1939 and was recruited by Al Capone's brother Ralph to work the Wisconsin lake gaming circuit, during which time he met his wife, Diana Mirick. Johnson fought in World War II and performed with the USO band, where Bob Hope gave him the nickname "Scat." (Courtesy of Leslie Johnson.)

Bobby Burdett is pictured playing saxophone in the first chair on the left. Burdett was one of the most beloved saxophone players in Milwaukee. He mentored Bunky Green and many other young musicians. According to local educator and activist Reuben Harpole, Lionel Hampton wanted to take Burdett on the road, but because Burdett had a weak heart, his mother did not want him to go. "That's why he stayed in Milwaukee," said Harpole, "otherwise he'd be really famous." Everett Clark is on the piano (left) and the trumpet player might be Holder Jones. (Courtesy of the Wisconsin Black Historical Society.)

Scat Johnson is pictured posing with his guitar. After World War II, Johnson moved to Milwaukee where he broke down barriers for black entertainers and performed regularly until his death in 1995. (Courtesy of Leslie Johnson.)

Claude Dorsey, pictured on the right, was born in Gainesville, Georgia. His family moved to Cincinnati and then to Milwaukee. Dorsey was playing professionally by the age of 12 with Bert Bailey and His Brown Buddies. Early in his career, Dorsey played in the Harold Robbins Orchestra and led a trio that became the house band at Dawson's Musicians Rest Nightclub. At Dawson's, Dorsey jammed with the likes of Roy Eldridge and Johnny Hodges. In the early 1940s, Dorsey and his band were gearing up for a move to Chicago, but the plans fell through. Shortly after, Dorsey took a gig at the Clock Lounge in downtown Milwaukee, which turned into a 35-year residency. Bill Stokes is pictured center. The drummer's name is unknown. (Courtesy of the Wisconsin Black Historical Society.)

The Count Carrington Trio is pictured performing at a club in the 1940s or 1950s. Carrington is on piano with John Graham on bass and Bill Stokes on saxophone. The singer's name is unknown. (Courtesy of the Wisconsin Black Historical Society.)

Pictured is the R&B group Harvey Scales and the Seven Sounds. On the far right is a young Rolla Armstead, who would go on to study jazz at the Wisconsin Conservatory of Music and become a noted saxophone player, including membership in the famous 10-piece CETA band alongside Sam Belton, Brian Lynch, Manty Ellis, Skip Crumby-Bey, Melvin Rhyne, Richard Chomick, and others. Al Vance is third from the left, another local jazz musician. Harvey Scales is in the white pants sixth from the left. (Courtesy of the Wisconsin Black Historical Society.)

A newspaper advertisement for Jack Rice and His Fine Trio is pictured here. In addition to leading his own group, Rice was featured in the Scat Johnson Quartet. For this gig at Thelma's Back Door, Rice's Trio was accompanied by Connie Milano, a boxer, bassist, and singer who gained notoriety in the Mil-Con-Bo Trio with pianist Siggy Millonzi and guitarist Don Momblow. Milano later ran the Crown Propeller Lounge in Chicago. (Courtesy of Milwaukee Jazz Vision.)

Milwaukee's Finest Black and Tan Cocktail Bar
THELMA'S BACK DOOR
Presents
FOR HIS 4TH SMASH WEEK
Jack Rice
AND HIS
FINE TRIO
Featuring

★ Everett 'Skip' CLARK
"Pianist with a Fine Future"

★ Eddie MEYERS
One of America's Top Swing
Violinists & Guitarists

Also
Vocalist Connie MILAN
Milwaukee's Own Song Stylist

Entertainment Every Friday, Saturday and Sunday Nites
MUSIC STARTS AT 9 P. M.

THELMA'S BACK DOOR
S. W. Corner of Juneau & N. 7th St. at
701 West Juneau Avenue

Iconic actor and singer Harry Belafonte is pictured hanging out at a jazz club in Milwaukee. The Harlem-born "King of Calypso" reached an international audience in the 1950s and popularized Caribbean music. Belafonte was an early supporter of the civil rights movement and has been an advocate for political and humanitarian causes throughout his life. (Courtesy of the Wisconsin Black Historical Society.)

Milwaukee entertainer Scat Johnson is pictured at right at a record-release celebration dinner for *Scat Johnson Sings* in January 1961. Johnson is seated next to two of the producers of the record, jazz legend Louis Jordan and local pianist Gladys Gaines, who also taught English in the public schools. The record featured local musicians Siggy Millonzi and Lester Harris. (Courtesy of Leslie Johnson.)

Legendary local blind organist Will Green is pictured playing with his signature pipe. Green owned a television repair shop and invented an instrument that wired bass pedals to an organ so they would sound like strings being plucked on a bass guitar, which he called the "T-Bass." Green was like a father to many local jazz musicians. Among his students were Marcus Robinson, David Hazeltine, and Neal Chandek. (Courtesy of the Wisconsin Black Historical Society.)

Roosevelt "Baby Face" Willette had his musical roots in the church. His father was a minister, and his mother played piano. Willette spent the early part of his career in gospel groups traveling around the United States, Canada, and Cuba. He took up jazz after moving to Chicago. In the 1950s, he lived in Milwaukee, where he played at the Flame, the Moon Glow, and Max's Tap, often alongside his singer wife, Jo Gibson. Willette moved to New York in 1960 and signed to legendary label Blue Note, recording two albums as a bandleader. (Photograph by Francis Wolff © Mosaic Images LLC, courtesy of Michael Cuscuna.)

"Wild" Bill Davison (left, on cornet) was born in the small town of Defiance, Ohio, in 1906. After living in Detroit and Chicago, Davison moved to Milwaukee in 1933 upon receiving an offer to lead a band at the Wisconsin Roof. Davison stayed in Milwaukee for seven years, playing at places like the Chateau Country Club, the East Side Spa, the Eagles Ballroom, the 26th and North Club, Schmitt's, and Lakota's. His main collaborators in Milwaukee were pianists Hilly Hansen and Gene Pairan and drummer Chic Hager. One of the last gigs Davison played in Milwaukee was at the Blatz Palm Garden, an elaborate dining room and nightclub in an old German hotel. Davison is pictured here in 1946 with Tony Parenti and an unidentified singer at Jimmy Ryan's club in New York City. (Courtesy of the Library of Congress.)

While he lived in Milwaukee, "Wild" Bill Davison often appeared at after-hours jam sessions in black nightclubs like the Moon Glow, where Jimmy Dudley led the house band. Davison once led a Saturday night jam session from midnight until dawn at a venue outside of town called Gesell's Grove. The first Saturday was so successful that the organizers did it again the next weekend, but the second time, it was shut down by the sheriff. (Courtesy of the Library of Congress.)

Davison's biographer Hal Willard describes "Wild" Bill's time in Milwaukee as "one long orgy of sex, alcohol, personal irresponsibility and fantastic music that was created in spite of the obstacles he placed in front of himself." Following his years in Milwaukee, Davison felt ready to try his hand in New York City. He found success in the jazz capital of the world and may be best known for his time at Eddie Condon's club in Manhattan. (Courtesy of Dewey Gill/Ray Sherman.)

Cladys "Jabbo" Smith was born in 1908 in Pembroke, Georgia. Following his father's death, Smith's mother sent him to an orphanage in Charleston, South Carolina, at age six. There, he learned to play the brass instruments. Smith often ran away and was expelled at 16. Not a year out of the orphanage, he joined the Charlie Johnson Band, during which time he turned down an invitation to join Duke Ellington's band. In 1928, Smith joined the touring show "Keep Shufflin'," alongside Fats Waller. After the tour, Jabbo moved to Chicago and played in several bands, including those led by Carroll Dickerson and Erskine Tate. (Courtesy of the Milwaukee Public Library.)

The Brunswick label recorded Jabbo Smith and His Rhythm Aces in an attempt to compete with Louis Armstrong, but promotion and sales were disappointing. From 1930 to 1936, Smith played with different bands in Milwaukee and Chicago. In 1938, Smith did the last recordings of his early career for the Decca label. He moved to Milwaukee in 1944, retired from music shortly thereafter, and worked at a rental car shop by the airport for years. In 1961, he was rediscovered and had a modest comeback in the United States and Europe. (Courtesy of the Milwaukee Public Library.)

Two

BIG BANDS

As jazz grew in popularity in the 1920s, bands expanded in size to become jazz orchestras. Mainstream dance bands and orchestras playing the Great American Songbook and other popular tunes also began to incorporate jazz elements. The 1920s through the 1940s is known as the big band era—also referred to as the swing era. Chicago, Kansas City, and New York served as the main hubs. Duke Ellington, Jimmy Lunceford, Fletcher Henderson, and Chick Webb were the best known black bandleaders. Tommy Dorsey, Jimmy Dorsey, Benny Goodman, and Glenn Miller were the biggest white bandleaders. Most big bands eventually gravitated to New York City because that was where the biggest stages and the majority of the recording studios were located.

In Milwaukee, Woody Herman emerged as a brilliant saxophonist and showman, playing around town as a teenager. Herman moved to Chicago, then New York, and later Los Angeles, becoming Milwaukee's best-known export of the big band era.

Bernie Young moved to Milwaukee from New Orleans in the 1920s and became the top black bandleader in town. Many of the best musicians in town got their start in Bernie Young's bands, including Jimmy Dudley, Bobby Burdett, and Leonard Gay. Other local black bandleaders included Eli Rice and Bert Bailey. Grant Moore and his New Orleans Black Devils were another band based in Milwaukee for some time.

There were four principal ballrooms in Milwaukee during the big band era: the Modernistic at the state fairgrounds, the Empire Room at the Hotel Schroeder, the Wisconsin Roof (also known as the Wisconsin Roof Garden) atop the Wisconsin Theater, and the Eagles Club Ballroom (also known as the "Million Dollar Ballroom" and later "Devine's Million Dollar"). In Hartford, the Chandelier Ballroom, run by Marty Zitco, was a popular destination for Milwaukee dance fans.

Cudahy native Vaughn Monroe left Wisconsin for college and formed a big band on the East Coast that would become one of the most popular of the post–World War II era.

In the 1950s, big band music began to decline as rock and roll and the bebop style of jazz emerged. Images in this chapter are from the 1920s through the 1950s, with special attention to those with Milwaukee connections.

This is a portrait of bandleader Bernie Young in 1940. Young was originally from New Orleans and became an active leader in the Milwaukee entertainment scene, including membership in the local black musicians union. (Courtesy of Paul Geenen.)

The Bernie Young Creole Band brass section is pictured in 1935. Manty Ellis remembers living down the block from Bernie Young in Bronzeville. Young held his band rehearsals right in his house. As a child, Ellis and his friends would walk over, listen in, and study the music of the Creole Band. (Courtesy of Paul Geenen.)

The Bernie Young Creole Band served as a stepping stone for many talented young musicians such as Jimmy Dudley, Ed Inge, C.T. Randolph, Mort McKenzie, and Leonard Gay. In 1923, the band recorded at a studio in Chicago for the Port Washington, Wisconsin–based label Paramount. (Courtesy of the Wisconsin Black Historical Society.)

The Bernie Young Works Progress Administration (WPA) Band is pictured in an unknown ballroom in the late 1930s. The WPA, renamed the Works Projects Administration, was the largest and most ambitious government agency to emerge out of the New Deal. The WPA employed millions of Americans during the Great Depression. (Courtesy of the Wisconsin Black Historical Society.)

Milwaukee native Mitchell Ayres (born Mitchell Agress) was a bandleader best known for his radio and television work with Perry Como and as conductor for the *Hollywood Palace* television show. Ayres attended Columbia University in New York City and began playing professionally at the Brooklyn Academy of Music. Shortly after graduation, he worked as a classical violinist in the Roxy Theater Orchestra and the St. Louis Symphony Orchestra but moved back to New York City to play jazz. Ayres worked with Jimmy Carr's Orchestra and later with Abe Lyman, Jack Little, Frank Sinatra, Benny Goodman, and Pearl Bailey. (Courtesy of Dewey Gill/Ray Sherman.)

Jazz icon Fats Waller famously played Milwaukee with a big band at the Blatz Hotel in 1942 shortly before he died. These performances could be heard across the country as remote radio broadcasts. (Courtesy of Historic Images.)

Pictured is the great bandleader Fletcher Henderson. The signature on the photograph reads, "To Bobby & Bernie, Two swell people," probably referring to Bobby Burdett and Bernie Young. Milwaukeean Jimmy Dudley once played with Henderson's band. (Courtesy of Paul Geenen.)

One of the unsung bandleaders of the 1930s, Eli Rice is pictured in front of his touring bus. Rice's orchestras were never recorded but had a strong reputation in the Midwest. (Courtesy of Paul Geenen.)

This advertisement for Bill Carlsen and the Original Wisconsin Roof Garden Orchestra is from the back of the August 24, 1929, issue of the Wisconsin Roof Garden's own *Rooftopic* publication. Carlsen was born in Clay Center, Kansas, in 1904. He attended the University of Wisconsin–Madison but left school to pursue music, touring with Isham Jones's band as a saxophonist. Carlsen came to Milwaukee in 1924 with Madison native Fred Dexter's orchestra. Carlsen took over Dexter's band in 1926 and played the Roof until 1931. He led bands at the Modernistic, the Futuristic at the Antlers Hotel, and the Schroeder Hotel. In 1951, he became a television meteorologist for WMTJ. (Courtesy of Dewey Gill/Ray Sherman.)

Pictured is the Wisconsin Roof Garden, nicknamed "the World's Wonder Ballroom," in June 1924 before its grand opening. It was operated by George Devine. After returning home from World War I, Devine opened the Chateau Club but changed the name to the Roseland. The Wisconsin Roof was atop the Wisconsin Theatre in the Carpenter Building on Wisconsin Avenue between Sixth and Seventh Streets. Devine was the nephew of the owner of the building, Jack Saxe. During the big band era, it was common for two bands to play opposite each other, as evidenced by the two bandstands in the picture. (Courtesy of Dustin Wittmann.)

Glen Lyte and the Midnite Serenaders are pictured in a park near Lake Michigan. Lyte, born Glen Lietzke, played on WTMJ radio broadcasts and at the Playland ballroom and the Eagles Ballroom. The Midnite Serenaders once played at the Eagles Ballroom opposite Sig Heller's band. Heller was another popular local bandleader who once played clarinet behind Louis Armstrong at the Schlitz Palm Garden. (Courtesy of Dustin Wittmann.)

STEVE SWEDISH

Steve Swedish was the leader of the pit band at the Riverside Theater, with 50 musicians working under him at its peak. The Wall Street crash hit Milwaukee in 1933, and the Riverside temporarily closed. Later, Swedish led a band at the Futuristic Ballroom during the cold months and the Modernistic Ballroom at the state fairgrounds during the mild months. Members of Swedish's orchestra included Gene Kuehnl, Harold Zuelsdorf, and Leslie Dietz. (Courtesy of Dewey Gill/Ray Sherman.)

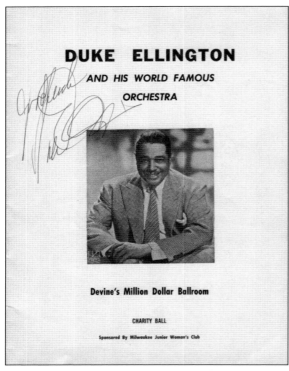

DUKE ELLINGTON

AND HIS WORLD FAMOUS
ORCHESTRA

Devine's Million Dollar Ballroom

CHARITY BALL

Sponsored By Milwaukee Junior Woman's Club

Pictured is a program for Duke Ellington and His World Famous Orchestra at Devine's Million Dollar Ballroom. For the length of the big band era, the ballroom only admitted white patrons. While Ellington and other black performers could perform at such venues, they were not allowed to stay in downtown hotels. Black entertainers were put up in Bronzeville at boardinghouses and with black families. (Courtesy of Dewey Gill/Ray Sherman.)

This is a press photograph featuring Duke Ellington and his orchestra from early in Ellington's career. At the time, the Washington, DC, native was represented by Mills Artists. When Ellington moved to New York City in the 1920s, he became a major figure in the Harlem Renaissance and the emerging jazz scene. (Courtesy of the Wisconsin Black Historical Society.)

The Eagles Club of Milwaukee opened in 1927 as a house for the Fraternal Order of the Eagles. It included a swimming pool, bowling alley, pool hall, barbershop, and a grand ballroom. In 1939, the venue was leased to George Devine and became known as Devine's Million Dollar Ballroom. The new proprietor booked famous big band jazz orchestras through the 1960s, after which it fell into disrepair. In the early 1990s, the building was purchased and renovated and is once again a major music venue in Milwaukee. (Courtesy of the Milwaukee County Historical Society.)

Tex Beneke and his big band featuring Jack Sperling on drums perform at Devine's Million Dollar Ballroom on May 8, 1946. On December 7, 1941, local bandleader Sig Heller and his group were playing a remote radio broadcast from the ballroom. The engineer gave them a signal to cut the performance short when news broke of the attack on Pearl Harbor that led to the United States' involvement in World War II. (Courtesy of the Milwaukee County Historical Society.)

Roland Bernard "Bunny" Berigan of Fox Lake, a town about an hour and a half outside of Milwaukee, never lived in the city. However, he surely influenced many local musicians in the 1930s and 1940s. Berigan was playing in a family band by age 12. His first professional gigs were with Merrill Owen and his Pennsylvanians, a quintet from the Fox Lake–Beaver Dam area. After graduation, Berigan moved to Madison, where he was based for a few years before moving to New York City. (Courtesy of the Harriet O'Connell Historical Room, Fox Lake Public Library.)

Music journalist Helen Oakley raved about Bunny Berigan after hearing him play at the Modernistic Ballroom in Milwaukee, writing that "only Louis Armstrong was comparable." Berigan's immense talent was often overshadowed by his reckless drinking, which led to him being kicked out of numerous bands and to his death at the age of 33. (Courtesy of the Harriet O'Connell Historical Room, Fox Lake Public Library.)

Bunny Berigan is pictured top left performing with the Tommy Dorsey big band. During his short but illustrious career, Berigan also played with bands led by Benny Goodman, Glenn Miller, and Eddie Condon. Early broadcasts of Benny Goodman's *Let's Dance* radio show in 1934, on which Berigan played, are said to have led to the development of the swing era. Some jazz historians cite the Palomar Ballroom show in Los Angeles at the end of Benny Goodman's 1935 tour as the beginning of the swing era, which Berigan played at. (Courtesy of the Harriet O'Connell Historical Room, Fox Lake Public Library.)

Bunny Berigan is pictured second from right at a jam session at WNEW radio station in New York City. Others pictured include Coleman Hawkins, Jack Jenney, Tommy Dorsey, Gene Krupa, Count Basie, and Martin Block. During his time in New York City, Berigan worked as a sideman for Billie Holiday and appears on some of her recordings. He also recorded with Louis Armstrong in 1936. (Courtesy of the Harriet O'Connell Historical Room, Fox Lake Public Library.)

Woody Herman was born in Milwaukee in 1913. His father was an amateur singer, and their family moved all over town. Herman began singing, dancing, and acting as a child. He learned the piano and saxophone, and started his musical career by playing saxophone in theaters around the Midwest. Herman was billed as "the Boy Wonder." While in high school, he played at the Blue Heaven Roadhouse, the Modernistic, and Pick's Madrid. The young Herman played with Joie Lichter's 10-piece group at the Strand Theater and, later, the Eagles Ballroom. When Herman played with Tom Gerun and His Orchestra at the Schroeder Hotel, he was offered a job and moved to Chicago in 1931, though the band was regularly on the road. Here, he is pictured seated playing the clarinet in the center with his band at Carnegie Hall in New York City in 1946. (Courtesy of the William P. Gottlieb Collection, Library of Congress.)

Woody Herman had become a celebrity by 1941, making appearances with his band on the silver screen. Herman and his wife bought a house in the Hollywood Hills from Humphrey Bogart and Lauren Bacall. Herman's Second Herd was named the top big band by *Down Beat* magazine in 1949 and did a fall tour with Nat King Cole. Despite the exciting music, money issues and drug use by some members led Herman to disband the Second Herd by the end of 1949. (Courtesy of the Historic Photo Collection/Milwaukee Public Library.)

The only Milwaukee weekly travel guide that is home owned, operated and printed in Milwaukee.

FEB. 19TH

WOODY HERMAN and his nationally famous orchestra now appearing in the Empire Room of the Hotel Schroeder.

The February 9, 1938, issue of local nightlife magazine *Goin' Places* features Woody Herman on the cover. Herman was in town to play the Empire Room in the Schroeder Hotel. Following the dissolution of the Second Herd, Herman continued to assemble bands and recruit rising talent, such as Latin jazz star Tito Puente and Wisconsin's own Dick Ruedebusch. Herman's Swingin' Herd backed famous singers like Mel Torme and Tony Bennett. Herman toured endlessly throughout his career, playing residencies at such venues as Caesar's Palace in Las Vegas and Disneyland in California. (Courtesy of Dewey Gill/Ray Sherman.)

Italian immigrant Joe Gumin began drumming as a child in Milwaukee in the 1910s. Gumin traveled all over the country playing in Dixieland big bands in the 1920s. Upon moving back home, he had an 11-year stint as the orchestra leader at Charlie Toy's restaurant on North Second Street. In 1947, Gumin's band cut a "Jingle Bells" record for which they sang in English, Polish, French, German, and Italian. A Gumin-led band is pictured here in 1953 at the Three Dolls, which was on the corner of North Third Street and Michigan Avenue. From left to right are Joe Gumin, Ralph Hildeman, Bill Ehlert, Art Laude, and Eddie Burleton. (Courtesy of Eric Hildeman.)

This advertisement for the Brass Rail is from the May 6, 1960, issue of *Goin' Places* nightlife magazine. The Brass Rail, at 744 North Third Street, was owned by the local mafia and booked some of the biggest names in jazz in the mid-1950s. By the late 1950s, the Brass Rail had primarily become a strip club with local musicians providing the soundtrack. This was true of most of the mafia owned venues in downtown, of which there were many. Joe Gumin's Orchestra is featured in this advertisement. (Courtesy of Dewey Gill/Ray Sherman.)

Mayville native Dick Ruedebusch was born in 1924. During World War II, he played in service bands and was stationed near New York City, which allowed him to sit in with big bands led by Gene Krupa, Jimmy and Tommy Dorsey, and Milwaukee's own Woody Herman. After the war, Ruedebusch went into the family business selling cars, but could not stay away from music for long. Upon moving to Milwaukee, he initially worked with Joe Gumin's band. Ruedebusch is pictured here in 1967, one year before his death, at the Tumblebrook Country Club in Waukesha County. From left to right are Ralph Hutchinson, Al Praefke, Don Eliot, Ruedebusch, and Chuck Hedges. (Courtesy of Historic Images.)

Pictured is an advertisement for Dick Ruedebusch's popular residency at the Tunnel Inn across from the Pabst Theater in downtown Milwaukee. Woody Herman brought Ruedebusch's band to New York City in 1962 and arranged an appearance on Ed Sullivan's Sunday night television program. Clarinetist Chuck Hedges was one of the brightest stars from the Underprivileged Five. A Chicago native, Hedges took a break from playing following the Tunnel Inn residency and worked as an instrument repairman. He experienced a career renaissance in the late 1970s, even touring Europe with "Wild" Bill Davison. Following his death in 2010, the Milwaukee nonprofit Jazz Unlimited has held annual concerts in Ruedebusch's honor. (Courtesy of Milwaukee Jazz Vision.)

Joe Aaron is pictured second from left at North Division High School, from which he graduated in 1937. Aaron was the youngest of six children and grew up in a Jewish neighborhood around North Avenue and North Fifteenth Street. His older brother Abe (born Alvin) was a renowned local reed player who started playing professionally in theater orchestras. After high school, Joe hit the road playing saxophone but moved back to Milwaukee in 1942 when his brother Abe joined Jack Teagarden's band. (Courtesy of Rick Aaron.)

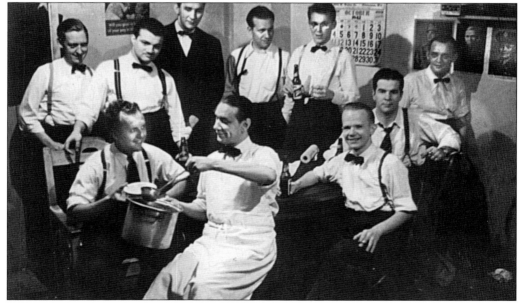

Upon joining Teagarden's band, Abe Aaron offered his little brother Joe his position in the Riverside Theater house band, which was a well-paying job at the time. Abe later became known for his three decades of work with Les Brown and His Band of Renown. Joe Aaron (second from left at top) is pictured backstage at the Riverside in the 1940s. (Courtesy of Rick Aaron.)

Joe Aaron is pictured at center blowing his saxophone and sporting a mustache. The player at lower left might be a young Claude Dorsey. At the time this photograph was taken, probably in the 1940s, it was rare for black and white musicians to mingle outside of after-hours clubs, where this may have been. Aaron went on to work in the Melody Top's orchestra, which staged musicals. He received work in the studio bands at local radio stations and with the WTMJ television orchestra. He was also hired by the Milwaukee Symphony Orchestra on the rare occasion that they needed a saxophonist. (Courtesy of Rick Aaron.)

Joe Aaron (third from right) is backstage at a performance in the 1940s. Trombone player Jimmy Birch is sitting on the bench. Aaron received a degree in music education from the Milwaukee State Teachers College, later the University of Wisconsin–Milwaukee. He went on to teach instrumental music and social studies at Juneau High School for 30 years. Aaron also taught privately and at the University of Wisconsin–Milwaukee. His students included local saxophonists Warren Wiegratz, Curt Hanrahan, and John Kirchberger. He continued to play with contemporaries like Sam Armato and Chuck Hedges until his death at age 93. (Courtesy of Rick Aaron.)

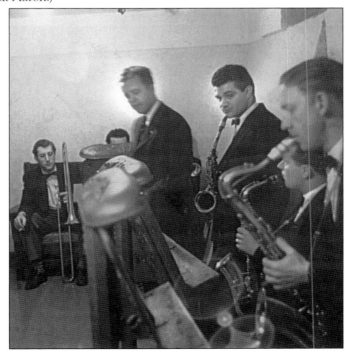

THE NEW YORK RECORDING LABORATORIES, Port Washington, Wisconsin

The Paramount record label, headquartered in Port Washington, was the best-known label in Wisconsin during the early 20th century. While Paramount specialized in the blues, the label ran the Broadway subsidiary, which recorded regional big bands in the 1920s and 1930s. There was a healthier market for jazz in Milwaukee than the blues during Paramount's peak. Paramount mainly leased studios in Chicago and New York City, but opened its own recording studio in Grafton next to its pressing plant in 1930. Pictured is a vinyl record of "River Boat Blues" by Devine's Roof Orchestra, led by Bill Carlsen. (Courtesy of Dewey Gill/Ray Sherman.)

Pictured is a handbill for the Modernistic Ballroom on the state fairgrounds. The Modernistic hosted dance bands until the early 1950s, when a massive snowstorm collapsed its roof. (Courtesy of Dewey Gill/Ray Sherman.)

Three

LOCAL LOVE

In the pantheon of Milwaukee jazz, there are many characters, some minor, some major. Figures in this chapter fall into three categories: those who grew up in Milwaukee and ventured out into the world, like Woody Herman and Al Jarreau; natives who spent most of their career in town, like Manty Ellis and Berkeley Fudge; and transplants like Hattush Alexander and Buddy Montgomery. No matter the qualification, each has played a part in the story of Milwaukee jazz.

Local drummer Dick Smith is remembered as one of the all-time greats. Smith was ahead of his time and never quite broke through to a national audience. Milwaukee has been home to many other notable drummers whose faces did not make it in this book, such as Bob Hobbs, Jimmy Duncan, Baltimore Bordeaux, Bob Budny, and Scott Napoli.

Some players only lived in Milwaukee for a brief period but left a lasting impact. Rahsaan Roland Kirk was chief among them. George Braith and Lonnie Smith also called Milwaukee home for a short time. Names that come up often but whose images could not be found include Pinky Black, Jimmy Talbert, Danny Reed, Carmen Weathers, Ronald Rideout, Holder Jones, and Barry Velleman.

In addition to those local musicians covered in the first two chapters and those pictured in the following pages, there are countless more that will live on in the memories of those who graced the scene.

Alwin Lopez "Al" Jarreau was born on March 12, 1940. He is pictured here at far right with his family. His father, a pastor, played the musical saw and won a top honor playing on the *Major Bowes Amateur Hour* radio program. Jarreau's mother played piano. He remembers hearing Ella Fitzgerald, Billy Eckstine, and Sarah Vaughan in his living room as a child. Jarreau started singing in church, at PTA meetings, and with friends in the streets and on the playgrounds of Milwaukee's north side. Jarreau attended Lincoln High School and studied Broadway music with Ron DeVillers. (Courtesy of the Wisconsin Black Historical Society.)

This newspaper clipping promoted pianist Les Czimber at the Driftwood Lounge in 1961. Czimber grew up in communist Hungary. He learned jazz music from listening to the *Voice of America* radio broadcasts and led a band in Budapest as a teenager. Czimber served in the Hungarian army during the 1956 revolution. He fled the turmoil in Hungary and moved to the United States, landing in Milwaukee, where he played with a young Al Jarreau for several years. Czimber and Jarreau continued to work together after moving to San Francisco. (Courtesy of Milwaukee Jazz Vision.)

After attending Ripon College, Al Jarreau played at the Driftwood Lounge and the Columns lobby lounge at the Pfister Hotel with Les Czimber. Following these formative years in town, Jarreau moved to California and went on to become Milwaukee's best-known jazz artist after Woody Herman. Jarreau was a multi-Grammy winning vocalist who could sing in multiple styles and regularly returned to play his hometown. He also lent his celebrity to a scholarship at his alma mater of Lincoln High School. (Courtesy of Historic Images.)

Jimmy Colvin was a native of Birmingham, Alabama, and a high school classmate of Herman "Sonny" Blount, better known as improvisational jazz pioneer Sun Ra. Colvin taught himself how to play the soprano saxophone and dropped out of college to pursue a career in music, hopping a freight train to New York City with hopes of making his mark in the Harlem jazz clubs. Colvin's first gig was with the Rhythm Maniacs. In the early 1940s, he played in the Bill Mason Trio, as well as his own combos. Colvin also filled in on sax when Louis Armstrong and Dizzy Gillespie needed a substitute. In the mid-1950s, he moved to Milwaukee. He continued to play jazz at night while running a dry cleaning business by day. Colvin later served as a police officer for 13 years. (Courtesy of Historic Images.)

Local pianist Loretta Whyte is pictured with Jimmy Colvin (right) and an unidentified man. (Courtesy of the Wisconsin Black Historical Society.)

The Jazz Old Timers rehearse for a television taping at the Wisconsin Conservatory of Music. From left to right are Victor Campbell on drums, Jimmy Colvin on saxophone, Jabbo Smith on trumpet, Al Washington on bass, and Loretta Whyte on piano. During his career, Colvin played in ensembles with fellow Birmingham native Jimmy Cheatham and his wife, Jeannie, who were influential jazz instructors at the University of Wisconsin–Madison in the 1970s. (Courtesy of the Wisconsin Conservatory of Music.)

Jimmy Colvin leads Milwaukee jazz icons Jabbo Smith and Loretta Whyte for the Jazz Old Timers taping at the PBS Channel 10 station in downtown Milwaukee. Not long after this performance, Colvin retired from his day job as a police officer and moved back to his hometown of Birmingham. During his career resurgence, Jabbo Smith moved to New York City and played until the age of 76. (Courtesy of Jamie Breiwick.)

Hattush Alexander, a St. Louis native, was a renowned saxophonist who regularly played at the Milwaukee Jazz Gallery. He first came to town with the Tommy Dean band in the 1950s; Alexander moved to Milwaukee shortly thereafter. He later taught at the Wisconsin Conservatory of Music and worked as a mailman. Chuck LaPaglia was inspired to open the Jazz Gallery after hosting Alexander and friends for a series of jam sessions at his house. (Courtesy of Milwaukee Jazz Vision.)

A native of Columbus, Ohio, Rahsaan Roland Kirk moved all over the Midwest during his 20s, landing in Milwaukee in 1959. Kirk lived above the Basin Street Lounge for three months. Basin Street was known for its Dixieland jazz shows, while Kirk was an experimental player. Kirk was born blind and primarily played tenor saxophone, though he could play various instruments and is known for playing several at once. (Courtesy of Historic Images.)

Frank Morgan was born in Minneapolis in 1933. He was raised by his grandmother in Milwaukee during the early part of his childhood and studied saxophone with Leonard Gay. In the late 1940s, during the advent of bebop, Morgan moved to Los Angeles to live with his father. Morgan, who was still a teenager, began playing saxophone in his father's after-hours club alongside bebop heavyweights Dexter Gordon, Wardell Grey, and the great Charlie Parker. Like Parker, Morgan became a heroin addict by age 17. He was arrested on drug charges following the release of his first record in 1955, shortly after Parker's death. (Courtesy of Charles Queen.)

Frank Morgan spent most of the years between 1955 and 1985 behind bars. In the early 1960s, he was a member of the all-star San Quentin inmate band alongside Art Pepper and Dupree Bolton. Morgan made a comeback in the mid-1980s and found success until his death in 2007, recording albums with such greats as McCoy Tyner, Wynton Marsalis, Barry Harris, and Bobby Hutcherson. In the 1990s, Morgan lived with Manty Ellis for nearly two years, which was not the first time the two Milwaukee jazz giants lived together. According to Ellis, Morgan's grandmother took Ellis's family in, and they grew up like brothers. (Courtesy of Pat Robinson.)

One of Chicago's most beloved Milwaukee imports, Willie Pickens was a world-class pianist who played internationally while mentoring and inspiring generations of Midwest musicians. Pickens grew up on North Sixth Street near Walnut Street, singing and dancing on the street and at the Lapham Park Social Center as a kid. He moved to Chicago in 1955 after graduating from the University of Wisconsin–Milwaukee. Pickens quickly became a prominent figure in the Windy City's illustrious jazz scene. (Courtesy of the *Milwaukee Journal Sentinel*.)

Vernice "Bunky" Green was born in Milwaukee in 1935. He learned from Bobby Burdett and played in clubs like Thelma's Back Door with Frank Foster of Count Basie's band. Like Willie Pickens, Green moved to Chicago as a young man after a brief stint with Charles Mingus's band in New York City. Green played on *The Steve Allen Show* and was admired by Cannonball Adderley. He became a renowned jazz educator in Chicago and later in Jacksonville, Florida. The same year he retired from teaching, 2011, Green appeared on the cover of *Down Beat* magazine with Rudresh Mahanthappa, with whom he had released a collaborative album called *Apex*. (Courtesy of Historic Images.)

Milwaukee's own Billy Wallace was of the same generation as Pickens, Green, and Manty Ellis, but Wallace was the eldest and considered the most skilled. He was self-taught and eventually moved to Chicago, where he became a noted player and teacher. One of his students was the great Herbie Hancock. Later, Wallace lived and played in Seattle, Las Vegas, and Denver. During his career, he played with Sonny Rollins and Max Roach. (Courtesy of Daniel Sheehan.)

Grover "Manty" Ellis was born in his family home on North Fifth and Vine Streets in 1933. His first memories of music were sitting on his father's lap while the elder Ellis played piano. As a child, Ellis and his friends sat in and listened to big band rehearsals led by Bernie Young and Bert Bailey. At age 13, Ellis heard Oscar Moore's guitar playing on a Nat King Cole song and decided to pick up the instrument. He studied with George Patrick at the Milwaukee Academy of Music, which was across the street from the Wisconsin Conservatory of Music. (Courtesy of Historic Images.)

Manty Ellis is pictured playing with Richard Davis in Milwaukee. Davis is a Chicago native who moved to Madison in the 1970s to teach at the University of Wisconsin–Madison. Davis and Ellis played together often during those years. Al Jarreau, a fellow Lincoln High School graduate, said of Ellis, "Manty became a really brilliant guitarist. Not many playing at that level, George Benson and a few others. Manty didn't get famous, but Manty was well known for his great work." (Courtesy of the Wisconsin Conservatory of Music.)

Manty Ellis (left) and Sonny Stitt are pictured performing in the back of a bar owned by Stitt's aunt and uncle. Stitt was originally from Michigan and visited Milwaukee often. He played saxophone in several big bands in the 1940s, replacing Charlie Parker in Dizzy Gillespie's bop big band in 1945. Stitt went on to play with Billy Eckstine, Chick Corea, Miles Davis, and Duke Ellington. Ellis briefly toured with the Stanley Turrentine big band alongside fellow Milwaukeean Vic Soward. He also lived in San Francisco in the late 1960s before returning home. (Courtesy of Howard Austin.)

Skip Crumby-Bey was raised in Boys Town, Nebraska, an orphanage for at-risk youth outside of Omaha. He learned to play piano as a child and began playing bass in the Army. Manty Ellis brought Skip to Milwaukee in the early 1970s. "When Skip came to town, everything changed," said Billy Johnson, Skip's former student. "He took everyone's job." Skip is pictured playing in the house band at the Milwaukee Jazz Gallery. (Photograph by TK Tearney, courtesy of Deborah Vishny.)

Milwaukee's own Berkeley Fudge is pictured in 1974. Fudge studied with Bunky Green, Willie Pickens, and Hattush Alexander. While attending North Division High School, his teachers assembled a jazz group that played together after school. As a young man, Fudge played in Leonard Gay's and Little Bo's big bands. His first band as leader featured John Elam on keys, Frank Gordon on trumpet, and Wendell Bond on drums. Fudge even employed an emcee who played trombone and told jokes between sets, as well as dancing from Satin Doll. As an educator, Fudge mentored generations of Milwaukee's jazz players. Local musician Kellen "Klassik" Abston studied with Fudge as a boy. "Our practices were a lot of call-and-response; he would play this super smooth, melodic jazz lick, and then I would have to play it back to him," said Abston. "He taught me how to listen, how to feel, how to let the chords dictate your phrasing." (Courtesy of Mark Davis.)

The Berkeley Fudge Sextet performs on a PBS Channel 10 Showcase. From left to right are Berkeley Fudge, Vic Soward, and Charles Davis Sr. Early in Fudge's career, he played in a band with Vic Soward and Mary Davis. He was also in a group with Gerald Cannon called the Elements. Davis Sr. came to town in 1948 from South Carolina and attended the Milwaukee School of Engineering. His son, Charles Davis Jr., became a noted tenor saxophone player in New York City. (Courtesy of Mark Davis.)

Local jazz stars Berkeley Fudge, Hattush Alexander, and Manty Ellis perform at the Pfister Hotel. While Fudge spent most of his career playing locally, he once toured with the Art Ensemble of Chicago in Europe. Alexander was in the original house band at the Milwaukee Jazz Gallery. All three taught together at the Wisconsin Conservatory of Music. (Courtesy of Howard Austin.)

Buddy Montgomery was born in 1930 in Indianapolis to a musically gifted family. His brother Monk became a pioneer of the electric bass, while Wes was a legendary guitar player. Buddy began on piano and added vibraphone to his repertoire in the 1950s. He played in the Seattle-based band the Mastersounds with Richie Crabtree and Benny Barth in the late 1950s. Crabtree later moved to Milwaukee and became a noted player. Jeff Chambers is pictured behind Buddy. Chambers, a Milwaukee native who studied at the Wisconsin Conservatory of Music, followed Buddy when he left town. (Courtesy of Mark Davis.)

Buddy Montgomery stayed in Milwaukee for almost a dozen years, working in town as a solo pianist and with smaller combinations. Noted band members include Jeff Chambers, Sam Belton, Andy LoDuca, and "Killer Ray" Appleton, another transplant from Indianapolis who lived in Milwaukee for some time. Buddy allegedly did not read music. Billy Johnson said Buddy considered it to be a totally aural art form. "Some of the older musicians said Buddy didn't even know the name of the note. He looked at it as a color or as a dimension or something geometric," said Johnson. (Courtesy of Historic Images.)

Pictured is a newspaper advertisement for Buddy Montgomery and Melvin Rhyne's residencies at the Bombay Bicycle Club in the Marc Plaza hotel and the Cafe Ole in the Pfister Hotel. The two Indianapolis natives were Milwaukee mainstays during the 1970s and early 1980s. Montgomery's residency, in particular, was attended religiously by young local musicians. Even big-name acts in town to play major ticketed shows would stop by the Marc Plaza and Pfister Hotel to watch these masters of the keys. (Courtesy of Milwaukee Jazz Vision.)

Indianapolis native Melvin Rhyne, born in 1936, is pictured at a recording studio in Milwaukee. Rhyne moved to Madison in 1969 and Milwaukee in 1973. A self-taught musician, he began his career playing piano with Rahsaan Roland Kirk, who also lived in Milwaukee for a period. In 1959, Rhyne teamed up with fellow Indianapolis musician Wes Montgomery. Rhyne may be best remembered for his playing on Wes Montgomery records for the Riverside label. He also played with blues legends B.B. King and T-Bone Walker. (Courtesy of Pat Robinson.)

Melvin Rhyne is pictured at center with Wendell Bond on drums and Berkeley Fudge on the left. Rhyne often played in Milwaukee with Fudge, David Hazeltine, and Brian Lynch. His organ of choice was the Hammond B3. Rhyne taught privately and as a musician-in-residence at Malcolm X Academy in 1995. In 1997, Rhyne and Manty Ellis were named winners of Jazz Master Awards from the prestigious Minneapolis-based foundation Arts Midwest. (Courtesy of Howard Austin.)

Adekola Adedapo, Melvin Rhyne, and Hattush Alexander perform at the Main Event, one of the hottest clubs in the post-1960s era. Rhyne lived in Milwaukee for over two decades before moving back to his hometown. Adedapo and Rhyne worked together regularly, including children's theater projects for the Inner City Arts Council. Adedapo has fond memories of working with Rhyne, who died on her 65th birthday. (Courtesy of Adekola Adedapo.)

Scat Johnson, known for his singing and guitar playing, poses at the drums for a photo shoot at the University of Wisconsin–Milwaukee with a group of young jazz players. From left to right are Thom Mason, Kaye Berigan, Johnson, Jim April, Mark Nevers, and Bill Schaefgen. Berigan and Schaefgen went on to be a part of the jazz fusion band What On Earth?, and Schaefgen composed a piece that the band played with the Milwaukee Symphony Orchestra in 1979. (Courtesy of Leslie Johnson.)

One of the best-known local guitarists, George Pritchett was an imposing and complicated character. Pritchett had a long-running duo with Don Momblow. He regularly played at the Brother's Lounge in the 1960s. In the 1970s, Pritchett's brothers owned a club at Landmark Lanes, where he often played. Pritchett gave guitar lessons at Metropolitan Music on North Avenue and Thirty-Sixth Street. Kinnickinnic Records was a short-lived local record label created exclusively to release two albums by Pritchett. While the jazz scene, like the city at large, was racially segregated, Pritchett often employed a black rhythm section that included Baltimore Bordeaux on drums, integrating otherwise all-white south side bars and clubs. (Courtesy of Historic Images.)

Tommy Sheridan was a native of Clinton, Iowa, who learned piano as a child in Catholic school. He became a professional piano player and performed around the Midwest. While on tour, he met Lorraine Wenkman in the late 1930s in Wisconsin Dells. The couple married and moved to Milwaukee shortly thereafter. Sheridan was playing at the Riverside Theater when he was scouted by Lawrence Welk. He spent a few years in Welk's band before deciding the road life was not for him. Sheridan became a popular bandleader and piano teacher in Milwaukee before moving to Wisconsin Dells in the early 1980s. (Courtesy of Historic Images.)

Kaye Berigan grew up on Milwaukee's East Side and is the nephew of legendary trumpet player Bunny Berigan. When he was a student at Riverside High School and the University of Wisconsin–Milwaukee in the 1950s, there were no jazz programs. Berigan cut his teeth at jam sessions in local clubs. He fondly remembers the Blue Monday Sessions run by trumpeter Billy Howell at a club on North Eighth and Walnut Streets, where he was one of the only white players to sit in. Berigan went on to have a lengthy career in small and big bands around Milwaukee and as a teacher in the public schools. (Courtesy of Kaye Berigan.)

Waukesha's Lester William Polfuss, better known as Les Paul, is a giant of American popular music. Though he is not considered a jazz musician by most standards, Paul's career was bookended by jazz, including parts of his early career and the last few decades of his life. Paul is the only person to be included in both the Rock and Roll Hall of Fame and the National Inventors Hall of Fame. Not only was Paul an accomplished country, jazz, and blues guitarist, he was also a pioneer of the solid-body electric guitar. (Courtesy of the Library of Congress.)

Though not known as a jazz artist, West Allis native Władziu Valentino Liberace, better known as Liberace, played piano and sang in Milwaukee jazz clubs early in his career. Liberace became the highest-paid entertainer in the world between the 1950s and 1970s. (Courtesy of Historic Images.)

Guitarist Jack Grassel was born in Milwaukee in 1948. He was a child prodigy on the accordion, inspired by Lawrence Welk's longtime accordion player and Milwaukeean Kenny Kotwitz. Grassel switched to guitar in high school during the advent of rock and roll. He was introduced to jazz by University of Wisconsin–Waukesha instructor Jack Whitney. Grassel began his teaching career at the Wisconsin Conservatory of Music and later designed the jazz program at Milwaukee Area Technical College, where he taught for 20 years. He continues to perform regularly with his wife, Jill Jensen. (Courtesy of the Wisconsin Conservatory of Music.)

Tommy Gumina was born in 1931 and grew up on Milwaukee's south side. He became a jazz accordion player and moved to Los Angeles. He performed on television shows hosted by Perry Como, Jackie Gleason, and Arthur Godfrey, and with Milwaukee's own Liberace. Gumina also started the successful Polytone Amps company based in California. (Courtesy of Historic Images.)

Scat Johnson is pictured (center) with his sons Mark (left) and Billy Johnson. According to his brother Billy, whenever Mark misbehaved his punishment was practicing the drums. Despite being left-handed, Mark plays a right-handed kit. As a teenager, he was playing in the house band at the Milwaukee Jazz Gallery. Both Johnson brothers studied in the Wisconsin Conservatory of Music's jazz program. Mark studied under Sam Belton before leaving for New York City on the insistence of legendary drummer Art Blakey. Mark immediately began working with Walter Davis Jr. and went on to play with Stanley Turrentine, Cassandra Wilson, Wallace Roney, and many more. (Courtesy of Leslie Johnson.)

As the son of Scat Johnson, Billy Johnson grew up in a musical household. His younger brother Mark played drums and was gigging with their dad early on. Young Billy preferred R&B and rock and roll, but once he showed interest in the upright bass, Scat sent him to study with Jimmy Johnson at Manty Ellis's music store. Later Billy studied with Skip Crumby-Bey and Mitch Kovic at the conservatory. He moved to New York City, where he has lived since, with stints back in Milwaukee. Billy has played with Lionel Hampton and Illinois Jacquet and with big bands based in New York. (Courtesy of the Wisconsin Conservatory of Music.)

Billy Johnson (bass) and Victor Campbell (drums) are pictured with pianist Ray Tabs. Tabs co-wrote and produced Milwaukee singer Penny Goodwin's album *Portrait of a Gemini*. Tabs and Goodwin held residencies all over town. Campbell was a student of the great Dick Smith and went on to play with Delfeayo Marsalis, Frank Morgan, George Braith, Carlos Santana, and others. Campbell also helped bring Roy Haynes to the Pabst Theater as part of their Hal Leonard Jazz Series that ran from 1993 to 2008. (Courtesy of Charles Queen.)

Milwaukee's jazz dentist, Seymour Lefco, is pictured with local singer Charlene Gibson. Lefco was friends with jazz musicians in town and treated big name players when they came through, including Oscar Peterson, Ray Brown, and George Shearing. He supported Gibson's career and later managed Milwaukee singer Penny Goodwin. Lefco even co-wrote some of the songs on Goodwin's *Portrait of a Gemini*. Later in his life, Lefco took piano lessons with Mark Davis, who currently directs the jazz program at the Wisconsin Conservatory of Music. (Courtesy of Historic Images.)

David
Hazeltine

Milwaukee-born pianist David Hazeltine first studied with the blind organist Will Green then later at the Wisconsin Conservatory of Music. Hazeltine played with Penny Goodwin after graduating from the jazz program. When the Milwaukee Jazz Gallery opened in 1978, he became a regular and often played with top national acts. The great Chet Baker encouraged Hazeltine to move to New York City, where he continues to play today. (Courtesy of the Wisconsin Conservatory of Music.)

Gerald Cannon is pictured on bass, with David Hazeltine on keys, Chris Harris on vocals, and Rick Krause on drums at Eddie Jackson's Supper Club in Bay View. Bassist Jeff Hamann studied with Cannon at the conservatory and described his teaching style as enthusiastic like a sports coach. Cannon, a Racine native, originally planned on being a gym teacher after college but was drawn to the jazz program at the conservatory. Cannon often played with Hazeltine and Penny Goodwin. Eventually, Cannon moved to New York City and worked with Roy Hargrove, Elvin Jones, and McCoy Tyner, and was even in the house band at the legendary Blue Note club. (Courtesy of Mark Davis.)

Milwaukee native Brian Lynch studied at the Wisconsin Conservatory of Music and went on to become a major trumpet player in New York City. He has worked in bands alongside jazz icons Art Blakey and Horace Silver. In 2006, the Brian Lynch/Eddie Palmieri album *Simpático* won the Grammy for Best Jazz Album. Berkeley Fudge, one of Lynch's teachers at the conservatory, said of Lynch, "I never knew Brian when he couldn't play. He could always play." (Courtesy of the Wisconsin Conservatory of Music.)

Carl Allen was born in Milwaukee in 1961. He grew up on gospel, R&B, and funk, but fell in love with jazz after hearing a Benny Carter record. His first hometown gigs were backing Sonny Stitt and James Moody. Allen studied at the University of Wisconsin–Green Bay and William Paterson University in New Jersey. Freddie Hubbard recruited Allen to join his band a year before graduation. Allen has played live and on record with Donald Byrd, Benny Golson, Bobby Hutcherson, Lena Horne, Art Farmer, J.J. Johnson, and many more. He is also an accomplished businessman and educator based in New York City. (Courtesy of Pat Robinson.)

Francisco Dominguez was born in Waukesha in 1931. He is a classically trained pianist who taught choral music in local schools while playing in clubs around town. Dominguez is better known by his stage name Frank DeMiles. One of his first gigs was with the saxophonist Zeb Billings in 1954, who opened a piano and organ store and released a series of successful organ lessons on cassette. DeMiles went on to play at the Holiday House. DeMiles and his wife had 11 children. Two of them, John and Peter, went on to have reputable careers in the jazz world. (Courtesy of Historic Images.)

Brookfield native Jeff Hamann began playing drums in grade school and later moved to bass guitar. Hamann studied with David Hazeltine at the Wisconsin Conservatory of Music and began playing out with his mentor immediately after graduation. He has since played with Charles McPherson, Slide Hampton, Frank Morgan, and Marlena Shaw, among others. For 18 years, he played bass on Michael Feldman's public radio show *Whad'ya Know?* out of Madison. When Feldman took the show on the road, Hamann played alongside James Brown's former drummer Clyde Stubblefield. (Courtesy of the Wisconsin Conservatory of Music.)

Claude Dorsey is pictured performing at the Clock Lounge on North Fifth Street off Wisconsin Avenue where he held a three-decade residency. Dorsey was once a substitute pianist when Billie Holiday played Milwaukee. He also jammed with Count Basie whenever he was in town. Dorsey was described as "Milwaukee's Own Nat King Cole." He had a rich baritone and delighted audiences with jazz, blues, and standards. In 2001, Dorsey was inducted into the Wisconsin Area Music Industry Hall of Fame. (Courtesy of Historic Images.)

Pictured is Milwaukee singer Jerry Grillo. A native of Hibbing, Minnesota, Grillo moved to Milwaukee in 1966 and taught for 30 years in the public schools. Grillo loves to sing standards, particularly of the jazz era. In the early 1990s, he went to local singer Jackie Allen for vocal coaching. Allen also helped Grillo set up his first recording in Chicago. (Courtesy of Jerry Grillo.)

Sigmund "Siggy" Millonzi was born in 1924 to an Italian family that lived on Milwaukee's East Side and later moved to Bay View. Millonzi was a child prodigy who studied classical piano at the Wisconsin Conservatory of Music. During World War II, he started an Air Force service band. Upon returning to Milwaukee, he began working as a jazz pianist. He is pictured at the piano with guitarist Don Momblow and bassist/singer Connie Milano, known collectively as the Mil-Con-Bo (also Mil-Combo) Trio. The group recorded an LP in 1955 for Capitol Records and went on to play two weeks at the iconic jazz club Birdland in New York City opposite the Stan Kenton Orchestra. (Courtesy of Stacey Vojvodich.)

Siggy Millonzi is pictured performing at Summerfest in the 1970s. According to Kaye Berigan, a Millonzi group in which Berigan was featured was the first to play the Miller Jazz Oasis in 1969. Millonzi also played at Summerfest with Berkeley Fudge and Manty Ellis, two of the top local black players. This is notable given the racial segregation of the Milwaukee jazz scene. For the 1971–1972 season of the Milwaukee Symphony Orchestra (MSO), Millonzi's trio and the MSO premiered his composition "Clairaudience." (Courtesy of Stacey Vojvodich.)

Siggy Millonzi is pictured (bottom) with Jack Carr (center) and Art Koenig. In the 1950s, Millonzi was a regular at Curro's in Milwaukee. He began playing with a sextet in the mid-1960s that included Walt Ketchum, Chuck Hedges, Ted Torcivia, and sometimes Hattush Alexander, Tony Pagano, and Kaye Berigan. Drummer Jack Carr is an Indianapolis native who played some of his earliest gigs in town with pianist Les Czimber and bassist George Welland at the Driftwood Lounge. While serving in the Army, Carr was stationed in his hometown and sat in with Indianapolis legends Wes Montgomery, Freddie Hubbard, and Slide Hampton. Upon moving back to Milwaukee, Carr began working with Millonzi and bassist Lee Burrows. Carr later joined big bands, most recently as a member of the Milwaukee Connection. Koening went on to lead his own groups and moved to New York City. (Courtesy of Stacey Vojvodich.)

Siggy Millonzi is pictured leading his big band at Club Garibaldi in Bay View, where the group played every Monday night from 1975 until Millonzi's death in 1977. He first formed a big band in 1968 for the inaugural Dick Ruedebusch Memorial Concert. Upon Millonzi's death, Jack Carr and Ron DeVillers took over the band. An all-day memorial concert was held at the grand ballroom on the seventh floor of the Pfister Hotel in honor of Millonzi, with a who's who of Milwaukee and Chicago players paying tribute. Art Koenig, who was then living in New York, debuted "Song for Sig" with Millonzi's big band at the memorial. (Courtesy of Stacey Vojvodich.)

Siggy Millonzi is pictured performing with a bandaged left hand in 1967. Art Koenig is on bass. According to the local newspaper, Millonzi jammed a screwdriver into his hand. At the time, he was working a lunch hour gig at Frenchy's restaurant on North Avenue and at night at the Grove on North Water Street. Millonzi was the rare Milwaukee jazz musician who made a living exclusively from playing music. Throughout his career, he played in Milwaukee, Chicago, and all over the country, backing jazz legends like Ella Fitzgerald, Sammy Davis Jr., and Sarah Vaughan. While Millonzi recorded for Capitol Records early in his career, he was one of the first Milwaukee jazz musicians to self-produce, releasing music under the Stacey Records label, which was named after his daughter. (Courtesy of Stacey Vojvodich.)

Four

SPECIAL LADIES

"I used to ask Martha [Artis] about the good ol' days," says Adekola Adedapo. "She said there were no good days. She wouldn't talk about the '40s and '50s. It was hard back then. Especially for black women in music."

There is no getting around the fact that jazz music, particularly in the early days, was a scene dominated by men. It is not easy for women to make it in jazz, especially for those who play an instrument. The day will come when female musicians are known simply as musicians, no qualifier required. But considering the hardship women have faced in the music industry, it seems fitting to dedicate a chapter to those who made a name for themselves in the Milwaukee jazz scene.

As mentioned in the opening chapter, Milwaukee's pioneering female jazz musician was Loretta Whyte. She blazed a path for future generations of local female musicians. Satin Doll was another icon of the scene who has been covered in previous pages. Some additional names from the early days include Mary Reed, Betty Landrum, Charlyn Smith, Betty Conley, Mary White, Mary Davis, and Brenda Smith. In the early 1980s, Adekola Adedapo was a part of an all-female jazz group that performed regularly at the Milwaukee Jazz Gallery.

Born in Milwaukee in 1928, Jackie Cain was a child prodigy singer. By 17, she was working with a commercial band that traveled around the Midwest and played regularly at a downtown club called Lakota's. Cain then moved to Chicago where she met her future husband, the pianist Roy Kral. The duo appeared on the 1956 television show *Stars of Jazz* and led a modestly successful career that included a residency in Las Vegas, commercial jingles, and tireless road work while raising two daughters. A New York critic described Cain as having "the jazz world's most underrated voice, pure liquid sound over voice."

Another notable Jackie born in Milwaukee, Jackie Allen is a vocalist who worked with the great Melvin Rhyne in the 1980s before moving to Chicago and starting her recording career. Allen has played all over the world and is a respected educator in Nebraska. Like Allen, Tierney Sutton is a Milwaukee-born jazz vocalist who found success outside of Wisconsin. The California-based singer has been nominated for several Grammys, one for a collaboration with Al Jarreau.

In the following pages appear some of the female jazz musicians who came to prominence in Milwaukee.

Milwaukee jazz icon Loretta Whyte performs in Milwaukee. Local musician Paul Cebar interviewed Whyte before her death at the age of 97. On her early playing in town with Tommy Fox's band, Cebar said, "To hear her talk about it you'd think it was Loretta Whyte and Her Clever Little Foxes!" (Courtesy of the Wisconsin Black Historical Society.)

A young singer named Gerry performs in Milwaukee. The back of the photograph reads, "To the fine and groovy person that I've met, you are right on the kick. To Archie, from Gerry." (Courtesy of the Wisconsin Black Historical Society.)

Born on Christmas Day 1919, Martha Artis was a regular in clubs around town and later taught piano and vocals in the jazz program at the Wisconsin Conservatory of Music. A teenage Manty Ellis learned the ropes by playing with Artis seven nights a week at a Walnut Street club called the Lounge. Artis is remembered for her warmth, humor, and improvised lessons. She is pictured here teaching a young student on piano. (Courtesy of the Wisconsin Conservatory of Music.)

Beverly Pitts is a Milwaukee native whose mother taught piano at the Tabernacle Baptist Church. Pitts learned jazz from a visiting musician in town from New York City. She played in the Elbow Room across from the Pabst Theater early in her career. Later in her life, when Pitts was quite ill, Neal Chandek organized a benefit at the Main Event that was well attended. (Courtesy of Justin Thomas Brown.)

Singer Jessie Hauck is pictured here. Hauck was recruited and brought to Milwaukee by fellow Springfield, Illinois, native Tony King, the architect of the jazz program at the Wisconsin Conservatory of Music. (Courtesy of the Wisconsin Conservatory of Music.)

Manty Ellis, Jessie Hauck, and Billy Johnson are pictured performing. Hauck became the principal jazz vocal instructor at the Wisconsin Conservatory of Music. Her classes were in high demand and regularly full. (Courtesy of Historic Images.)

Berkeley Fudge, Manty Ellis, and Jessie Hauck perform at a private event at the Pfister Hotel. While teaching at the conservatory, Hauck stayed busy working gigs all over the Midwest. She often worked as a duo with Manty Ellis, who remembers Hauck as a "phenomenal singer." (Courtesy of the Wisconsin Conservatory of Music.)

Jessie Hauck is pictured at center smiling at the Peck Pavilion outside the Marcus Center for the Performing Arts. She was a regular at the Milwaukee Jazz Gallery and is remembered for her incredible vocal range and quality of character. (Courtesy of Charles Queen.)

Penny Goodwin began singing in church with Al Jarreau, at weddings, talent competitions, and bat mitzvahs. She sang in town at clubs such as Sardino's, the Pfister Hotel, and King's IV before moving to clubs in Chicago and Las Vegas. She recorded the album *Portrait of a Gemini* with the Ray Tabs Trio. The record featured co-writing and financing by Milwaukee's jazz dentist Seymour Lefco. (Courtesy of 88Nine Radio Milwaukee/WYMS Vinyl Archive.)

Pictured is a press photograph of Milwaukee singer Marcia Cunningham from 1968. Cunningham was in an R&B group with local musicians Marcus Robinson and Charles Small. She sang at Sardino's, the Milwaukee Jazz Gallery, and many other venues in town. (Courtesy of Historic Images.)

Milwaukee native Charlene Gibson is pictured performing with Manty Ellis at the Crown Room atop the Pfister Hotel. When Barbara Jean Love of the R&B group Friends of Distinction took time off during her pregnancy, Gibson moved to California and replaced her, singing on some of the group's biggest hits. (Courtesy of Historic Images.)

Juli Wood is pictured at right on saxophone with the Milwaukee band the R&B Cadets. Wood was introduced to jazz while on an exchange program in Germany. She later studied with David Hazeltine and Berkeley Fudge, earning a performance degree from the University of Wisconsin–Milwaukee. Wood sings and plays baritone, soprano, alto, and tenor saxophone. Others pictured from left to right are Rip Tenor, Al Anderson (bass), Robin Pluer, Paul Cebar (guitar), and Randy Baugher. (Photograph by Francis Ford, courtesy of Paul Cebar.)

Tina Moore was a pioneering black model who loved to sing jazz but did not start playing out until later in her life. Moore began singing at the same time she and her husband, Boobie, opened Jamie's Club Theater on North Thirty-Fifth Street off West Capitol Drive. Boobie had previously owned a club called Boobie's Place. At lower right is the jazz musician and artist Alvin Junior. (Courtesy of Tina Moore.)

Connie Grauer and Kim Zick went to the same high school in Waukesha but rarely spoke to each other. Years later, Zick formed a band and called Grauer, who she recalled was a piano player. Together, they formed MRS. FUN in Nashville, where they lived for five years before moving back to Milwaukee. (Courtesy of Connie Grauer.)

MRS. FUN is pictured performing at Teddy's (now Shank Hall) on Milwaukee's East Side. The duo had a popular residency at the Cafe Melange inside the Hotel Wisconsin during the 1990s. In the early 1980s, Zick played drums in an all-female ensemble alongside Adekola Adedapo at the Milwaukee Jazz Gallery. MRS. FUN continues to perform today. (Courtesy of Connie Grauer.)

Adekola Adedapo was born in Chicago in 1948 and raised there until age six. Her grandfather owned a bar on the South Side where Adedapo recalls listening to jazz singers on the jukebox as a young girl. Adedapo then moved to Muskegon, Michigan. She moved to Milwaukee in 1973, then relocated to the Oyotunji African Village in South Carolina in 1975, returning to Milwaukee in the late 1970s. She began her singing career while working in the public schools. In the 1980s and early 1990s, she lived in Chicago and worked with Von Freeman and Bobby "Slim" James. Adedapo returned to Milwaukee in 1994. Her daughter Naima was a contestant on the 10th season of the popular television show *American Idol.* (Courtesy of Adekola Adedapo.)

Milwaukee native Sonya Robinson is pictured on stage with Willie Pickens on piano and Berkeley Fudge on saxophone. Robinson is a graduate of Nicolet High School and the University of Wisconsin–Milwaukee. She was crowned Miss Black America in 1983. Miles Davis allegedly compared her playing to legendary jazz violinists Ray Nance and Stuff Smith. (Courtesy of Adekola Adedapo.)

Five

LEGENDS LIVE

Being only a short drive or train ride from Chicago, Milwaukee has been hosting the biggest names in jazz for a century. Cab Calloway, Fletcher Henderson, Jimmy Dorsey, and Benny Goodman all played Milwaukee in the 1920s and 1930s. Louis Armstrong played the Schlitz Palm Garden consecutive summers early in his career. Duke Ellington has probably played Milwaukee the most over the years. Dizzy Gillespie and Lionel Hampton also played Milwaukee across the decades.

It is important to note that in the first half of the 20th century, visiting black entertainers, even the biggest names in music, could play downtown venues but could not stay in most downtown hotels because of racist policies. Therefore, black musicians often stayed in rooming houses or with families in Bronzeville, the black community north of downtown.

One of the most talked about shows in Milwaukee jazz history—in which a young John Coltrane played with Miles Davis's All-Star Quintet in March 1959 at the Brass Rail—never actually happened. Bobby Tanzillo debunked this mythical show in an article for OnMilwaukee.com. The show was scheduled but fell through for mysterious reasons. However, Coltrane, Davis, and fellow Quintet member Cannonball Adderley all played Milwaukee over the years. Coltrane played the Riverside Theater with Dizzy Gillespie as a young man in the 1950s. Herbie Hancock's first professional gig was in Milwaukee at Curro's in 1960, which Bobby Tanzillo also wrote about in detail for OnMilwaukee.com.

The images in this chapter reveal a sampling of the jazz royalty that has delighted Milwaukee audiences over the years.

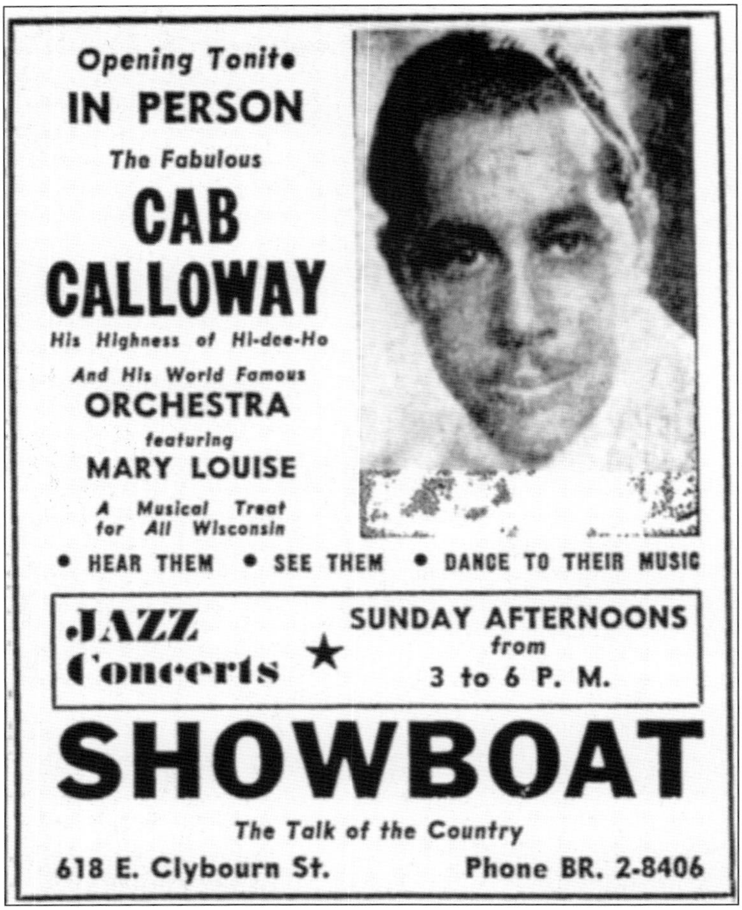
Opening Tonite
IN PERSON
The Fabulous
CAB
CALLOWAY
His Highness of Hi-dee-Ho
And His World Famous
ORCHESTRA
featuring
MARY LOUISE
A Musical Treat
for All Wisconsin
• HEAR THEM • SEE THEM • DANCE TO THEIR MUSIC
JAZZ
Concerts
SUNDAY AFTERNOONS
from
3 to 6 P. M.
SHOWBOAT
The Talk of the Country
618 E. Clybourn St.
Phone BR. 2-8406

An ad for Cab Calloway's performance at the Showboat is pictured here. Calloway led one of the most popular big bands of the 1930s and 1940s, playing numerous times in Milwaukee. (Courtesy of Dewey Gill/Ray Sherman.)

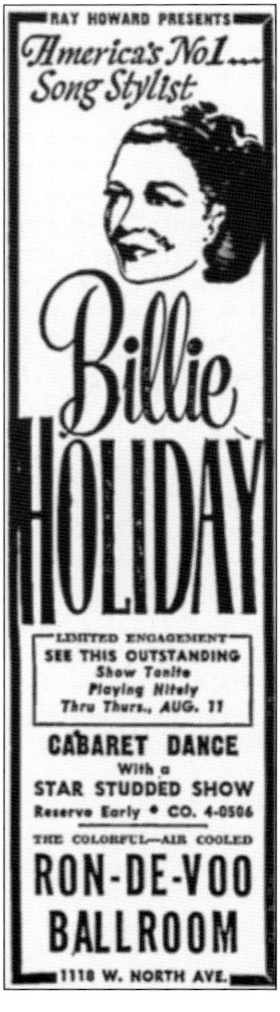
RAY HOWARD PRESENTS
America's No1...
Song Stylist
Billie
HOLIDAY
LIMITED ENGAGEMENT
SEE THIS OUTSTANDING
Show Tonite
Playing Nitely
Thru Thurs., AUG. 11
CABARET DANCE
With a
STAR STUDDED SHOW
Reserve Early • CO. 4-0506
THE COLORFUL—AIR COOLED
RON-DE-VOO
BALLROOM
1118 W. NORTH AVE.

This ad was for the great songstress Billie Holiday's four-night engagement at the Ron-De-Voo Ballroom on North Avenue in August 1953. Berkeley Fudge remembers the Ron-De-Voo as a place that regularly hosted wrestling matches. (Courtesy of Milwaukee Jazz Vision.)

Born Ruth Lee Jones in Tuscaloosa, Alabama, Dinah Washington was one of the most popular black female singers of the 1950s. Her family moved to Chicago when she was a child, where she began performing in clubs at the age of 15. Between 1948 and 1955, Washington had 27 R&B top-10 hits, recording with premier jazz musicians such as Cannonball Adderley and Ben Webster. Here, she is pictured performing at a club off North Avenue and Humboldt Avenue on Milwaukee's East Side. (Courtesy of the Wisconsin Black Historical Society.)

Lionel Hampton (left) performs in Bronzeville in the 1940s. The jazz icon spent the early part of his childhood in Kenosha, Wisconsin, before his family moved to Chicago. Hampton helped popularize the vibraphone in 1930 after Louis Armstrong had him play the instrument on a recording. (Courtesy of the Wisconsin Black Historical Society.)

Count Basie and Joe Williams are pictured performing at the Brass Rail in 1958. Basie's band included 17 musicians for the one-night-only performance. (Courtesy of Historic Images.)

Louis Jordan and his Tympany Five are pictured playing at the Brass Rail. The club was on the same block as Curro's and Gallagher's, making up a Third Street trio that hosted some of the biggest names in jazz during the 1950s and early 1960s. Manty Ellis remembers one night when Ahmad Jamal was playing at Gallagher's, and Oscar Peterson was next door at Curro's. (Courtesy of the Wisconsin Black Historical Society.)

Chicago native Gene Krupa was photographed by Donald Emmerich using a triple exposure technique. Krupa was one of the first superstar drummers and an icon of the big band era. One of his earliest visits to Wisconsin was in 1937 at the Modernistic at the state fairgrounds with Benny Goodman's band. Twenty years later, in March 1957, Krupa's own band played a week-long run at the Brass Rail. Despite a heavy snowstorm on opening night, a packed house turned out and was delighted by Krupa's powerhouse drumming. (Courtesy of the *Milwaukee Journal Sentinel*.)

This advertisement for J.J. Johnson at Curro's appeared in the May 6, 1960, issue of *Goin' Places*. Johnson, an Indianapolis native, worked with Miles Davis, Max Roach, Tommy Flanagan, and Cedar Walton throughout his illustrious career. (Courtesy of Dewey Gill/Ray Sherman.)

— LIMITED ENGAGEMENT —
Monday, May 9th Thru Sunday, May 15th

J. J. JOHNSON and his SEXTET

America's Foremost Jazz Trombonist
★ ★ ★
Coming May 20 - 28 . . . . Jack Teagarden

CURRO'S SHOW LOUNGE
821 - 27 N. Third St. — 1 1/2 Blocks North of Wisconsin Ave.

Dave Brubeck is pictured at the piano in concert at the Performing Arts Center. Brubeck was a prominent figure in the West Coast cool jazz style. (Courtesy of Historic Images.)

Oscar Peterson is pictured performing at Milwaukee Area Technical College. The legendary jazz pianist was born in Montreal in 1925 and led a distinguished 60-year career. (Courtesy of the Historic Photo Collection/ Milwaukee Public Library.)

Arthur "Art" Blakey, later known as Abdullah Ibn Buhaina, was a Pittsburgh native and iconic drummer. He started playing in the 1940s with big bands led by Fletcher Henderson and Billy Eckstine, helped establish bebop with Thelonious Monk, Dizzy Gillespie, and Charlie Parker, and formed the Jazz Messengers with Horace Silver in the 1950s. The Jazz Messengers became an incubator for young talent. The first time the Marsalis brothers played Milwaukee, it was with Art Blakey. Here, Blakey is pictured at the Top of the Inn in the Holiday Inn Midtown. (Courtesy of Howard Austin.)

Donald Byrd, a Detroit native, is pictured (right) being interviewed by Mike Drew of the *Milwaukee Journal*. Byrd was a major trumpet talent who played Milwaukee often during his career. Drew was an entertainment critic who covered jazz in town for many years. (Courtesy of Howard Austin.)

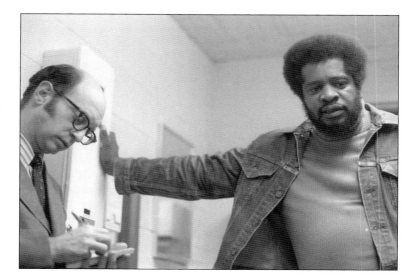

Chicago native Herbie Hancock is pictured at the piano. Hancock studied with Milwaukee native Billy Wallace as a child and played his first professional gig at Curro's in Milwaukee with Donald Byrd's band, about which Bobby Tanzillo has written for OnMilwaukee.com. (Courtesy of Kevin Lynch.)

In 1975, following a nearly half-century career in music, Woody Herman returned home to Milwaukee to set up the Sister Fabian Riley scholarship fund for young musicians. The fund honored the teacher who inspired and encouraged Herman the most in his youth. (Courtesy of Dewey Gill/Ray Sherman.)

Six

MUSIC IN THE AIR

The most beloved venue for live music in Milwaukee is not contained within four walls. For over a century, Milwaukeeans have had a special adoration for music outdoors. Whether under a blazing sun or in the dark of the moonlight, jazz musicians have been heard outside since John Wickliffe and his Famous Ginger Band first performed at Schlitz Garden in 1916.

Summerfest on the shores of Lake Michigan is the granddaddy of outdoor music venues in Milwaukee, hosting jazz musicians since its inception in 1968. The Miller Jazz Oasis stage opened soon after on the Summerfest grounds. In recent years, jazz has had its own day at Henry W. Maier Festival Park. The Jazz Visions on the Lake series is a collaboration between Summerfest and Milwaukee Jazz Vision that began in 2013.

While jazz has been held at various outdoor festivals around town, calls for an exclusively jazz festival began in the 1960s. As a result, the Milwaukee County Jazz Galaxies Festival took place at County Stadium in the 1970s and featured the Pointer Sisters, Donald Byrd and the Blackbyrds, Stanley Turrentine, McCoy Tyner, and the Akiyoshi-Tabackin big band.

One of the longest-running outdoor festivals in town is the Lakefront Festival of Art outside the Milwaukee Art Museum on Lake Michigan. In the 1970s, the festival included some of the biggest names in jazz, including Dizzy Gillespie and Elvin Jones. The Alewives Festival hosted the Buddy Montgomery Quintet in the 1970s. In recent decades, Jazz in the Park and Bastille Days have hosted top-notch jazz in downtown's Cathedral Square Park.

Pictured is the original main stage at Summerfest, now known as "the World's Largest Music Festival." The striped tent on the right is the Miller Jazz Oasis. The iconic Hoan Bridge, named after the socialist mayor who served from 1916 to 1940, can be seen above the Jazz Oasis tent. (Courtesy of the Milwaukee County Historical Society.)

The Miller Jazz Oasis is pictured on the right. Many legendary performers graced this stage during its years as a showcase for jazz. This photograph was likely taken from the Skyglider ride that carries festival-goers above the grounds. (Courtesy of the Historic Photo Collection, Milwaukee Public Library.)

Buddy Montgomery and a group perform at Summerfest in the 1970s for a PBS Channel 10 television crew. Hattush Alexander is on the saxophone. (Courtesy of the Historic Photo Collection/ Milwaukee Public Library.)

Skip Crumby-Bey (left) and Berkeley Fudge are pictured performing at Summerfest at the Miller Jazz Oasis. Manty Ellis first saw Crumby-Bey perform in Milwaukee with a couple from Florida in the 1960s and was blown away by his skills on the bass. Ellis and Crumby-Bey jammed at an after-hours club and Ellis got Crumby-Bey's phone number. In 1970, Ellis called Crumby-Bey, who had grown tired of living and playing in New York City, and sent Crumby-Bey a ticket to come to Milwaukee. Upon moving to town, Crumby-Bey became a highly influential player and teacher. (Courtesy of Jamie Breiwick.)

Elvin Ray Jones of Pontiac, Michigan, became a well-respected jazz drummer of the post-bop era. He came to prominence while playing with John Coltrane in the 1960s. Racine-born, Milwaukee-trained musician Gerald Cannon was the last bassist to play in Jones's band. Cannon told the writer Kevin Lynch, "I learned more about dynamics, time, groove, and melody from Elvin than any band I had ever played with before him." Jones is pictured playing at the Lakefront Festival of Art. (Courtesy of Howard Austin.)

Carmen McRae and her band perform at the Washington Park Bandshell as part of the Kool Jazz Festival in 1982. Other performers included Dizzy Gillespie, Mel Torme, Gerry Mulligan, George Shearing, Freddie Hubbard, the Heath brothers, Akira Tana, and Sarah Vaughan. (Courtesy of Jamie Breiwick.)

The legendary Louis Armstrong is pictured performing at the Wisconsin State Fair in 1968. Armstrong performed in Milwaukee numerous times during his career, including consecutive summers at the Schlitz Palm Garden. (Courtesy of the *Milwaukee Journal Sentinel*.)

Pictured from left to right at the Washington Park Bandshell are percussionist Dumah Safir, Adekola Adedapo, singer Joe Jordan, singer Brenda Smith, Vic Soward, an unidentified dancer, Melvin Rhyne, organist Mary Davis, Berkeley Fudge, and singer Diana Bradford, with Andre Lee Ellis crouching at center. Safir appeared on all of Melvin Rhyne's records and recorded with Otis "Killer Ray" Appleton, an Indianapolis transplant who lived in Milwaukee for a time. (Courtesy of Adekola Adedapo.)

John Birks "Dizzy" Gillespie was one of the greatest jazz innovators of all time. In the 1940s, Gillespie was a major figure in the development of bebop. The trumpeter played Milwaukee a number of times throughout his career, including the Riverside Theater. Here, he is pictured speaking with fans at the Lakefront Festival of Art. (Courtesy of Howard Austin.)

Marian McPartland was an English-American pianist, composer, and writer. From 1978 to 2011, she hosted her own jazz program on National Public Radio. The Grammy lifetime achievement award winner regularly toured the world and was even named to the Order of the British Empire. Here, she is pictured in 1972 performing at Milwaukee's Lakefront Festival of Art. (Courtesy of Howard Austin.)

Buddy Montgomery leads a group at the Alewives Festival in the 1970s. The downtown arts festival was put on by the Performing Arts Center and named after a type of silver-colored fish that had been washing up on the shores of Lake Michigan. It was the predecessor to the Live at Peck Pavilion series. (Courtesy of Mark Davis.)

Local musicians perform at a street festival outside of Jamie's Club Theater in the late 1980s. The street festival is a staple of summer in Milwaukee and is a prime avenue for young musicians and veterans to reach a broader audience. (Courtesy of Tina Moore.)

Local Latin jazz group La Chazz performs at an early version of Jazz in the Park. From left to right are Dave Bayles, Hector Rodriguez, Bob Siegel, Toty Ramos, Luis Diaz, Allan Johnson, Jeff Pietrangelo, Neal Chandek, and Mike Franceschi. La Chazz began playing cha-chas for ballroom dancing with a Puerto Rican rhythm section and later became more jazz-oriented. The group played with the Milwaukee Symphony Orchestra in 1981, held a residency at the Wisconsin Hotel, and played at La Playa atop the Pfister Hotel (formerly the Crown Room). La Chazz was also the first band to play the inaugural Bastille Days. (Courtesy of Charles Queen.)

Berkeley Fudge looks back at the camera during a Jazz in the Park performance at Cathedral Square. The contemporary series has become a downtown Milwaukee favorite. (Courtesy of Charles Queen.)

Seven

THE SPOTS

Considering the lifespan of a live music venue is generally short, it can be difficult to track all the places in Milwaukee that have hosted jazz. In the early days, hotels and ballrooms were the main places to see live jazz. While most activity was in and around downtown, community halls and gymnasiums in far-flung neighborhoods were hiring jazz bands for dancing as early as the 1920s. Clubs soon sprouted up in downtown and Bronzeville.

After-hours clubs and bars became hot spots for late night jam sessions. This is where many of the city's white and black performers mingled after their official paying gigs. While most clubs were located downtown and in the Bronzeville neighborhood, on the south side there were some ballrooms and a few clubs by the 1950s, including the Continental, Stage Door, and Club Carnival.

High school auditoriums and college campuses became common places for jazz fans to see some of the bigger names of the bebop generation in the 1950s through the 1970s. For example, legendary drummer Max Roach played at the University of Wisconsin–Milwaukee in 1957 and Ahmad Jamal played a standing-room-only show at the Shorewood Auditorium.

By the late 1960s, Bronzeville was broken up by a freeway project, and many jazz clubs either shut down or became isolated. Only a few places in town remained dedicated to live jazz. In the 1970s, hotels came back around as one of the few places to regularly host jazz, including the Marc Plaza and Pfister Hotel.

The Riverside and Pabst Theaters in downtown have been hosting jazz for most of their respective histories. A few iconic clubs operated during the latter part of the 20th century, including Teddy's, the Jazz Oasis, the Main Event, and the Jazz Estate.

Nellie Wilson (center) was one of the premier hostesses who worked at the Flame and the Moon Glow. Here, she is singing with a couple of jazz players at the Polk-A-Dot, which was operated by Derby Thomas, who also ran the Flame. (Courtesy of Aaronetta Anderson/Paul Geenen.)

The Brass Rail owner Izzy Pogrob (left) is pictured with, from left to right, Dottie Smith, unidentified, and Louis Jordan. Pogrob was allegedly murdered by the mob in 1959 for stealing a boxcar of their alcohol. Organized crime was heavily involved in the entertainment business during this time and owned more than 10 clubs in and around downtown. (Courtesy of the Wisconsin Black Historical Society.)

The cover of the May 24, 1947, issue of *Goin' Places* nightlife magazine is pictured. The names of numerous local clubs are scattered across the cover. (Courtesy of Dewey Gill/Ray Sherman.)

When the Performing Arts Center opened alongside the Milwaukee River in 1967, it became a hot spot for jazz fans. It includes four major theater venues, including the open-air Peck Pavilion. (Courtesy of Historic Images.)

A Wisconsin Conservatory of Music jazz ensemble performs with members of the Milwaukee Symphony Orchestra at the Performing Arts Center. The group is led by Tony King and includes, from left to right, John Foesheger, John High, Irv Quartman, Gerald Cannon, and Scott Preston. (Courtesy of the Wisconsin Conservatory of Music.)

The Crown Room atop the Pfister Hotel hosted national acts and local performers between 1966 and 1981. Local bassist George Welland began his playing career with Les Czimber and Jack Carr at the Pfister Hotel. Welland went on to lead the house band at the Crown Room, playing with legends like Billy Eckstine. The space later became La Playa in 1981 and Blu in 2000. Though the venue is smaller in size, it continues to host live jazz in a sophisticated, intimate setting. (Courtesy of the Marcus Corporation Archives.)

Pictured is the exterior of the Pfister Hotel in 1974. The circular Pfister Tower opened in 1966, with the Crown Room (now Blu) located at the top. (Courtesy of Historic Images.)

Pictured is Sardino's nightclub along Farwell Avenue on Milwaukee's East Side. The club was a remnant of mid-century mafia-owned jazz clubs and booked top local talent. Owner Frank Sardino's brother Joe owned another club called the Bull Ring that was an important place for the explosion of jazz fusion in the 1970s. (Courtesy of Charles Queen.)

Kenneth P. Gerlat, also known as "Dr. Feelgood," is pictured in front of the Jazz Riverboat, which he owned and operated. The venue was located at 2718 North Riverboat Road. It was a popular place for live music in the mid-1970s, specializing in New Orleans–style jazz and food. When the Jazz Riverboat went out of business, Gerlat opened the Blue Note at 1339 East Brady Street. Gerlat was a musician himself and occasionally sat in during jam sessions at his clubs. (Courtesy of Historic Images.)

One of Milwaukee's most beloved modern jazz venues, which continues to operate, the Jazz Estate is located in a former residential house and tavern on the East Side. Neal Chandek and Dave Glasser first played a duo for tips and made it such a popular spot that local businessman Sal Monreal bought the place in the late 1970s and turned it into a dedicated jazz club. (Courtesy of Charles Queen.)

Pictured is the building that housed Manty Ellis's music store from 1972 to 1992, at 1912 West Hampton Avenue. It was a little retail shop with a small stage where Ellis practiced and held rehearsals. As word spread, the store became a hangout for national artists in town on a gig. "I had some of the best music come out of the store that you can't even get recordings of," said Ellis. "People like Freddie Hubbard, Frank Morgan, Eddie Harris, Sonny Stitt. You might come up to the store and find George Benson sleeping on my couch." (Author photograph.)

Opened in the late 1970s, Satin Doll's Lounge closed its doors sometime in the 2000s when its namesake Minette "Satin Doll" Wilson went into a nursing home. The author has driven past the club countless times going from his parents' house in Sherman Park to downtown and always wondered what had transpired inside. In 2008, Talking Heads frontman David Byrne visited the club and wrote, "The room was filled with Christmas decorations, faded photos of Doll with Duke and some more recent soul singers, stuffed animals and Milwaukee police patches." (Author photograph.)

A mural for Caroline's Jazz Club is pictured on the side of a daycare on North Forty-Ninth and Burleigh Streets, up the road from where the author was raised. Caroline's is located in the historic Walker's Point neighborhood at 401 South Second Street, near the author's residence when he completed this book. Caroline's opened in 2000 and has been a staple of the contemporary jazz scene. (Author photograph.)

Eight

THE CONSERVATORY

Jazz has always been an art form built on apprenticeship. Joe Oliver taught Louis Armstrong. Billy Wallace taught Herbie Hancock. When Walnut Street and the surrounding spots were jumping, any kid with an instrument could go from club to club and try to impress the veterans, in hopes that someone might show them the ropes. That became less possible as the clubs spread out and grew more isolated. Luckily, in 1971, Manty Ellis and Tony King founded the jazz program at the Wisconsin Conservatory of Music.

The jazz program at the conservatory is one of the longest running in the nation. It was originally an accredited college program and attracted instructors from New York and Chicago. Student ensembles of the late 1970s swept competitions at the Elmhurst and Notre Dame festivals. The program played a pivotal role in the Milwaukee jazz renaissance of the late 1970s and early 1980s.

Tony King was the architect of the program. "Tony King is like the genius of our time," exclaims Manty Ellis. "He was the most amazing person I've ever met in my life. Anything you wanted to talk about or ask him about, he could tell you. Music was his favorite subject. The guy was just blowing my head open with information about music and theory."

One year, the judges at the Elmhurst Jazz Festival included Dizzy Gillespie. When it was time for the judges to perform, the festival tapped the conservatory jazz ensemble's rhythm section. Gillespie later came to the conservatory to give a workshop. Most of the bright stars of the last 50 years of Milwaukee jazz passed through the halls of the conservatory, which sits in a historic building on Prospect Avenue overlooking Lake Michigan.

Because of the conservatory jazz program, apprenticeships moved from informal friendships to a formal educational setting. As a result, the demographics of the Milwaukee jazz scene in the post-1970s era shifted from mostly black musicians to a more affluent, more white crop of students and players.

The exterior of the Wisconsin Conservatory of Music is pictured here. It is located at 1584 North Prospect Avenue. The conservatory is descended from two music schools founded in 1899, the Wisconsin College of Music, originally located in Mendelssohn Hall across the street from the Central Library, and the Wisconsin Conservatory of Music, originally housed in the Ethical Building on Jefferson Street facing Cathedral Square. The two schools merged in 1971. The building was originally a mansion built by industrialist Charles McIntosh in 1903. (Courtesy of the Wisconsin Conservatory of Music.)

A postcard from the jazz program at the Wisconsin Conservatory of Music is seen here. The jazz program was founded in 1971, the same year that the two schools merged to become the conservatory. The program offered an accredited four-year degree in jazz. (Courtesy of the Wisconsin Conservatory of Music.)

Tony King is pictured teaching a young woman on the piano. King and Manty Ellis designed the jazz program at the conservatory, which was a three-year process. King was a native of Springfield, Illinois. He attributed his hunger for knowledge to the Jim Crow segregation he endured as a child in southern Illinois. (Courtesy of the Wisconsin Conservatory of Music.)

Tony King is pictured teaching at the Wisconsin Conservatory of Music. "The human mind tolerates what gives it pleasure, and what gives it pleasure is what it can do without thinking," is a quote from King often recited by former students. (Courtesy of the Wisconsin Conservatory of Music.)

Tony King is pictured holding his daughter Shirley. When King moved to Milwaukee, he became friends with Scat Johnson, Everett Clark, and Jack Rice. He toured all over the state until he and Ellis came up with the jazz program, and then King dedicated his life to teaching. (Courtesy of the Wisconsin Conservatory of Music.)

Tony King is pictured receiving an award. Manty Ellis does not remember King playing much during his years as an educator. "He would play a couple of notes, then people would congregate around the piano and he'd started espousing on this and that," said Ellis. (Courtesy of the Wisconsin Conservatory of Music.)

Brian Lynch is pictured (left) with headphones in the conservatory listening room. (Courtesy of the Wisconsin Conservatory of Music.)

An award-winning conservatory jazz combo is pictured here. Standing from left to right are Manty Ellis, Brian Lynch, Charles Small, Marcus Robinson, Harry Kozlowski, Rolla Armstead, and Jeff Chambers. Sam Belton is seated. Belton was a student at Rufus King High School with Vic Soward when they started playing in R&B bands. As a kid, Belton learned from a public school drum instructor named Roy Schneider. Belton studied classical percussion and jazz and then became a teacher at the conservatory. He now operates City.Net Jazz Café in downtown Milwaukee. (Courtesy of the Wisconsin Conservatory of Music.)

Guitarist Ted Dunbar gives a master class at the conservatory for jazz students. Dunbar, a Texas native, worked as a substitute for Wes Montgomery in the 1960s and went on to become a respected educator at Rutgers University, where he taught Vernon Reid and Kevin Eubanks. (Courtesy of the Wisconsin Conservatory of Music.)

A row of jazz students studies at the Wisconsin Conservatory of Music. (Courtesy of the Wisconsin Conservatory of Music.)

Instructor Marth Artis teaches a young woman at the conservatory. Artis taught vocal and piano lessons. (Courtesy of the Wisconsin Conservatory of Music.)

Eddie Baker (right) moved to Milwaukee from Chicago to teach in the jazz program at the conservatory. Baker was a Kansas City native committed to preserving the jazz legacy through music education. He was a vocal advocate for creating a jazz hall of fame, which eventually led to the opening of the American Jazz Museum in his hometown. (Courtesy of the Wisconsin Conservatory of Music.)

A conservatory student combo is pictured in Room 5 in the basement of the conservatory. From left to right are Rolla Armstead, John Zaffiro, Harry Kozlowski, Marcus Robinson (seated), Mark Johnson, Brian Lynch, and Al Anderson. (Courtesy of the Wisconsin Conservatory of Music.)

John High (left) and Brian Hendrick are pictured performing at the conservatory. (Courtesy of the Wisconsin Conservatory of Music.)

Manty Ellis is pictured (center) with two students in the former dining room at the conservatory. At left is drummer Roland Rutkoswki. (Courtesy of the Wisconsin Conservatory of Music.)

Manty Ellis instructs a student combo in a rehearsal room at the conservatory. From left to right are Bill Krumberger, Irv Quartman, John High, John Foesheger, Scott Preston, Gerald Cannon, and Rodney Simpson. (Courtesy of the Wisconsin Conservatory of Music.)

The conservatory jazz program staff is pictured around 1977; from left to right are Eddie Baker, Manty Ellis, Jesse Hauck, Berkeley Fudge, Jeff Pietrangelo, Scott Preston, and Reggie Willis. Pietrangelo was allegedly so skilled at reading music that after subbing with the Russian Circus, they made him an offer to join the touring company. (Courtesy of the Wisconsin Conservatory of Music.)

The conservatory jazz program staff ("We Six") is pictured in the 1990s; from left to right are Dave Bayles, Berkeley Fudge, Mark Davis, Mike Plog, Jeff Hamann, and Paul Silbergleit. (Courtesy of the Wisconsin Conservatory of Music.)

Nine

THE GALLERY

The jazz program at the Wisconsin Conservatory of Music was a major factor in the resurgence of Milwaukee's jazz scene in the 1970s. Another critical component was Chicago native Chuck LaPaglia opening the Milwaukee Jazz Gallery on East Center Street in September 1978. With Teddy's converting to a discotheque in 1975, the Milwaukee Jazz Gallery filled the gap by bringing in top-level jazz acts.

LaPaglia brought his experience and connections with the Chicago scene to the Milwaukee Jazz Gallery. LaPaglia's friendship with Milwaukee saxophonist Hattush Alexander was integral to his decision to open the club. Kathleen Connelly, a friend from the University of Wisconsin–Milwaukee, helped set up the business end. The building was a tavern and adjacent wedding hall built in the 1880s.

With a background in social justice and community work, LaPaglia was committed to serving a diverse clientele at a reasonable price. Another part of his mission was to combine Chicago and Milwaukee musicians. The Milwaukee Jazz Gallery was undoubtedly a jazz club, but LaPaglia also booked blues, folk, and some alternative acts, including the Violent Femmes, one of Milwaukee's best-known musical exports.

During the Gallery's six-year run it became one of the best clubs in the country, hosting icons like Chet Baker, Dizzy Gillespie, Stan Getz, and the Marsalis brothers. Journalist Kevin Lynch regularly covered the Gallery for the *Milwaukee Journal*. "That was a *happening* jazz club," Lynch wrote. "I remember many bands transmitting enormous energy. It felt like an intelligent life-force carrying meaningful form with beauty, drama, wit and mystery."

The conservatory jazz program had a close relationship with the Gallery. Students attended jam sessions and master classes at the Gallery. Some, like 19-year-old David Hazeltine, got to sit in with legends like Sonny Stitt. Milwaukee trumpeter Brian Lynch first played with Art Blakey at the Gallery and was later hired by the iconic drummer.

LaPaglia lived above the Gallery, and his kitchen was the de facto green room. Many local musicians have fond (if somewhat hazy) memories of hanging in the kitchen. The kitchen is where LaPaglia said the best informal education was given.

The Gallery hosted benefit events for local community groups and also collaborated with nearby Woodland Pattern Book Center on an avant-garde series that brought The Chicago Art Ensemble and Sun Ra to Milwaukee. Following the Gallery's run, LaPaglia moved to Oakland and booked jazz at Yoshi's nightclub.

Detroit vibraphone legend Milt Jackson is pictured performing at the Jazz Gallery. One night Jackson was playing the Gallery, a summer storm took out the electricity. The band then went upstairs to play cards. The crowd refused to leave, hoping it could be fixed. When LaPaglia realized it was not possible, he convinced Jackson to finish the night playing by candlelight. With no electricity to amplify the vibraphone, the crowd had to be completely silent. LaPaglia remembers it as one of the more magical evenings at the Gallery. (Photograph by TK Kearney, courtesy of Deborah Vishny.)

Milwaukee native Willie Pickens is pictured performing at the Jazz Gallery. Pickens joined the Army after high school and played the clarinet in the service band. After moving to Chicago and switching to piano, he played in the Eddie Harris band in 1961. Thirty years later, Pickens was recruited to tour and record with the Elvin Jones Jazz Machine. Throughout his career, Pickens accompanied Sammy Davis Jr., Wynton Marsalis, Charlie Parker, and Quincy Jones. He mentored countless students including Kenny Anderson of the Ohio Players and Michael Harris of Earth, Wind & Fire. Pickens died of a heart attack in 2017 immediately following a rehearsal at Jazz at Lincoln Center in New York City. (Photograph by TK Kearney, courtesy of Deborah Vishny.)

Chuck LaPaglia grew up in Chicago, worked with street kids, joined the Army, was stationed outside of New York City, and developed a lasting love of jazz. He even played a little himself. LaPaglia moved to Milwaukee in 1969 for a position at the University of Wisconsin–Milwaukee. A series of jam sessions at his house with Hattush Alexander coupled with a mysterious dream is what convinced LaPaglia to make his own jazz club a reality. (Courtesy of Milwaukee Jazz Vision.)

Milwaukee native Bunky Green (right) is pictured performing with Sonny Stitt at the Jazz Gallery. These happen to be two of Berkeley Fudge's heroes. (Photograph by TK Kearney, courtesy of Deborah Vishny.)

Milwaukee's best-known rock and roll export, the Violent Femmes, are pictured in a press photograph from the 1980s. From left to right are Gordon Gano, Brian Ritchie, and Victor DeLorenzo. The group played at the Jazz Gallery and continues to incorporate jazz elements in their music. During the grand opening concert at the Fiserv Forum in downtown Milwaukee in 2018, the home of the NBA's Milwaukee Bucks, the Violent Femmes opened for the Killers and brought out local saxophonist Aaron Gardner during their set. DeLorenzo left the band in the 2000s but is based in Milwaukee and continues to perform in the duo Nineteen Thirteen. (Courtesy of Historic Images.)

Violent Femmes lead singer and Rufus King High School graduate Gordon Gano is pictured (left) with the great organist Melvin Rhyne. In April 1982, one could go to the Gallery on a Tuesday night and see the Violent Femmes for $2 and then come back the next night to see the Mel Rhyne Trio for $1.50. (Courtesy of the *Milwaukee Journal Sentinel*.)

Celebrated guitar player and Pittsburgh native George Benson is pictured playing at the Jazz Gallery. Benson was a child prodigy who came to prominence in the 1960s. He was a celebrated session player employed by the likes of Miles Davis, Freddie Hubbard, and Stanley Turrentine. (Photograph by TK Kearney, courtesy of Deborah Vishny.)

Bebop saxophone player and Newark native James Moody is pictured playing at the Jazz Gallery. "I'll never forget the exchange [I had] with James Moody," said Adekola Adedapo. "He told me, 'Baby just take your time. Always let the band play until you hear what you need to hear and then go.' It was the best piece of advice I could've got." (Courtesy of Historic Images.)

Iconic jazz singer and Detroit native Betty Carter is pictured performing at the Jazz Gallery. Carter was known for her improvisational singing style and her incorporation of scatting. Her big break came in 1948 when she was asked to join Lionel Hampton's band. She had an illustrious solo career and worked with Miles Davis, Sonny Rollins, and Ray Charles, among others. (Photograph by TK Kearney, courtesy of Deborah Vishny.)

Marsalis brothers Branford (left) and Wynton, pictured here in the early 1980s, first performed in Milwaukee with Art Blakey and the Jazz Messengers at the Jazz Gallery. Adekola Adedapo remembers hanging out with the band upstairs and giving Wynton Marsalis an "Ileke" necklace to protect him from negative influences and energies. (Courtesy of Historic Images.)

Ten

IN TIME

In the second half of the 20th century, rock and roll, funk, soul, disco, R&B, hip-hop, and electronic music each became entrenched in popular culture. As a result, jazz was relegated to the margins of the music industry. But as local guitarist Manty Ellis points out, "Everything on the radio that's making money is related to what they call 'jazz,' it's almost the standard of the world." Indeed, jazz provided the foundation for American popular music. In recent years, jazz has experienced a resurgence thanks to stars like Kamasi Washington and Esperanza Spalding. Milwaukee's own music renaissance of the mid-2010s was partly due to musicians rooted in jazz.

Jazz has stayed vital in Milwaukee thanks to a number of institutions, organizations, and individuals. The Milwaukee Jazz Society of the early 1960s was credited for jumpstarting the career rebirth of Jabbo Smith. The nonprofit Jazz Unlimited of Greater Milwaukee has been promoting jazz since 1971. The Milwaukee Jazz Experience in the mid-1980s provided in-school performances, workshops, panel talks, and concerts. Journalists like Rich Mangelsdorff and Mike Drew offered coverage in local publications, while radio DJs like Ron Cuzner and Howard Austin spread the message over the airwaves.

A number of talented jazz artists have emerged out of Milwaukee in recent decades. Dan Nimmer is a gifted pianist who was hired by Wynton Marsalis to join the illustrious Jazz at Lincoln Center Orchestra in 2005. Before becoming a prominent member of the New York City jazz scene and moving to Paris, bassist Joe Sanders grew up and trained in Milwaukee. Rick Germanson is another Milwaukee expat who made his mark on the New York City scene. Guitarist extraordinaire Angie Swan fondly recalls jam sessions at Caroline's as a teenager. In addition to the Wisconsin Conservatory of Music, the West End Conservatory has become another incubator of young talent.

"Jazz asks you to be proficient with your instrument, to know it well, to study it like a classical player so that it's a part of your hands or lips," says Milwaukee jazz legend Al Jarreau.

"Okay, now that you know it, come and be free. Make your statement. Improvise. You know the changes and the melody, now make a new melody.

"That's a calling that will always be inviting to a young musician."

Milwaukee writer Kevin Lynch is pictured interviewing the singer Asha Puthli. Puthli was in town singing with Henry Threadgill, the Chicago native and Pulitzer Prize–winning composer. (Courtesy of Kevin Lynch.)

Ron Cuzner was a radio DJ, columnist, record store owner, and jazz promoter in Milwaukee for many years. Cuzner could be heard on a variety of stations, typically opening his program with the following introduction: "Ron Cuzner is my name. I bring you America's music, America's poetry. Syncopated, of course. Often improvised. And usually modulated. In a word, jazz." Digital archives of Cuzner's shows can be listened to as a podcast. (Courtesy of Charles Queen.)

Howard Austin is originally from Detroit and attended high school with legendary Detroit musicians like Donald Byrd. He moved to Milwaukee in the early 1970s and worked as a radio DJ at WUWM and later WYMS. Austin also hosted jazz events in town, including the Kool Jazz Festival at the Washington Park Bandshell in 1982. In addition, Austin was a photographer and contributed a number of photos to this book. (Courtesy of Charles Queen.)

Berkeley Fudge (left) is pictured with Charles Queen, a member of the Milwaukee Jazz Experience and a visual artist. Queen was a strong supporter of local jazz and contributed photographs to this book. (Courtesy of Charles Queen.)

Russ Johnson is one of the most accomplished jazz musicians living in Milwaukee. A Racine native, he began driving up to Milwaukee and down to Chicago to see jazz as soon as he got his driver's license. As a young man, he sat in at jam sessions at the Jazz Estate. Johnson spent two decades playing in New York City before moving back to the Midwest for a professorship. (Photograph by Weston Rich, courtesy of Jay Anderson.)

Jamie Breiwick is a celebrated educator, consummate performer, and primary contributor to Milwaukee Jazz Vision, a website dedicated to promoting the local jazz scene past and present. The Racine native has shared the stage with Milwaukee R&B icon Eric Benet, jazz luminaries David Hazeltine and Ralph Bowen, and beloved local groups Clamnation and Choirfight. Breiwick's tireless dedication to the jazz scene also includes graphic design work for show posters and album and book covers. He continues to perform with a variety of combinations including Lesser Lakes Trio, Kase, and Dreamland. Breiwick's work has been essential to the realization of this book. (Courtesy of Jamie Breiwick.)

Foreign Goods is pictured at Tonic Tavern during Bay View Jazz Fest 2016. Foreign Goods is a super group led by saxophonist Jay Anderson. The band features a rotating combination of players from various styles and influences rooted in jazz. Foreign Goods is emblematic of the Milwaukee music renaissance of the mid-2010s. From left to right are (first row) Quentin Farr, Sam Gehrke, Britney "B~Free" Freeman-Farr, Abby "Abby Jeanne" Gurn, Kyndal "Kyndal J" Johnson, and Kellen "Klassik" Abston; (second row) Michael Anderson, Tim Russell, Jay Anderson, and Randy Komburec. (Courtesy of Jay Anderson.)

Augie Ray is Milwaukee's "jazz superfan" and an ambassador of the Jazz Unlimited nonprofit organization. Ray has been attending shows since the 1950s. Here, he is pictured on the right at Blu atop the Pfister Hotel, wearing glasses and laughing. David Hazeltine is at the piano, Mitch Shiner is on drums, and Jeff Hamann is on bass. (Courtesy of Leiko Napoli.)

DISCOVER THOUSANDS OF LOCAL HISTORY BOOKS FEATURING MILLIONS OF VINTAGE IMAGES

Arcadia Publishing, the leading local history publisher in the United States, is committed to making history accessible and meaningful through publishing books that celebrate and preserve the heritage of America's people and places.

Find more books like this at
www.arcadiapublishing.com

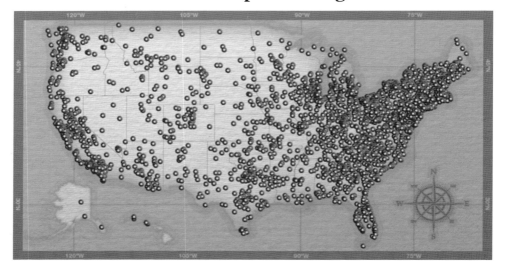

Search for your hometown history, your old stomping grounds, and even your favorite sports team.